DAVID JONES

THE TATE GALLERY

ISBN 0 905005 03 1 paper 0 905005 08 2 cloth
Published by order of the Trustees 1981
for the exhibition of 21 July – 6 September 1981
Copyright © 1981 Paul Hills

Published by the Tate Gallery Publications Department,
Millbank, London SW1P 4RG
Designed by Sue Fowler
Printed by Balding + Mansell, Wisbech, Cambs

This catalogue is set in Monotype Joanna – a typeface
drawn by Eric Gill in 1930 and produced for machine
composition by Monotype in 1937

CONTENTS

7 Foreword

9 Acknowledgements

11 List of plates

13 Chronology

19 The art of David Jones Paul Hills

72 Catalogue

    Engravings & printed illustrations 72
    Boxwood carvings 77
    Drawings & paintings 79
    The inscriptions of David Jones Nicolete Gray 127
    Manuscripts 140

141 Bibliography

143 List of lenders

Cover/jacket: The Farm Door 1937
Frontispiece: David Jones at Harrow in 1965;
taken for his 70th birthday (Photo: Mark Gerson)

FOREWORD

David Jones belongs to that line of British poet-painters, so exceptional to our culture, of which Blake and Rossetti are the great exemplars. An exhibition can only show a part of his achievement, but that part is substantial.

This is the second David Jones exhibition at the Tate Gallery – the first, arranged by the Welsh Committee of the Arts Council in 1954–5, will still be well remembered by all those who saw it. It was an impressive occasion, and we hope to repeat its success with this retrospective, the first major exhibition of the work of David Jones since his death in 1974. Paintings, drawings and inscriptions are included, together with some engravings and boxwood carvings. The writings, constantly referred to in the catalogue, are represented by a small display of manuscripts.

We are extremely grateful to Dr Paul Hills, Lecturer in History of Art at Warwick University, for selecting the exhibition and for writing the catalogue. We should also like to thank Mrs Nicolete Gray for advising on the selection of inscriptions and for writing this part of the catalogue.

No exhibition can take place without the generosity and support of owners, public and private. Some names are mentioned in the catalogue, but many lenders have preferred to remain anonymous. To them all, however, we extend our sincere thanks. We have borrowed extensively from several collections and we are particularly grateful to the David Jones Trustees, to Douglas Cleverdon and to Nicolete Gray, and to the National Library of Wales and the National Museum of Wales.

When the exhibition closes at the Tate it will be shown at the Graves Art Gallery, Sheffield from 19 September until 18 October, and then at the National Museum of Wales, Cardiff from 31 October until 13 December.

Alan Bowness
Director

ACKNOWLEDGEMENTS

This exhibition has been made possible by the generous help of very many people. I owe a special debt to the Trustees of the Estate of David Jones who have aided my research over many years; to Nicolete Gray, who has advised about the choice of many items and especially the painted inscriptions, for which she has also written the catalogue entries; and to Douglas Cleverdon, who has shared with me his unrivalled knowledge of David Jones's engravings. Anthony d'Offay and Caroline Cuthbert at the Anthony d'Offay Gallery have been particularly generous with their time and energy.

I should like to thank Faber and Faber Ltd for permission to reprint extracts from In Parenthesis, The Anathemata, The Sleeping Lord, The Dying Gaul by David Jones and Dai Greatcoat: A Self-portrait of David Jones edited by René Hague.

I should also like to thank for help of many kinds, David Blamires, Tom Burns, Nest Cleverdon, Philip W. Davies, Mrs Catherine Dupré, Arthur Giardelli, Peter Guy, Father John Hagreen, Thomas Hodgkin, Edgar Holloway, Stanley Honeyman, Miss Jacqueline Hope Wallace, Sir Antony Hornby, Christopher Hull, Mrs A.K. Jackson, Malcolm Jones, Mrs N.B.L. Lucas, Peter Orr, David Pryce-Jones, Mrs Denis Tegetmeier, Julian Watson, and Mrs Valerie Wynne-Williams. Finally, I am grateful to Caroline Odgers of the Tate Gallery for her unfailing support.

Paul Hills

LIST OF PLATES

17 THE WATERFALL, AFON HONDDU FACH 1926
[Cat. no. 37, p. 83]

18 JULY CHANGE 1929
[Cat. no. 61, p. 90]

27 CATH GARTREF 1930
[Cat. no. 68, p. 92]

28 PIGOTTS FARM 1930
[Cat. no. 70, p. 94]

29 PLACE FOR SHIPS 1931
[Cat. no. 79, p. 96]

30 MANAWYDAN'S GLASS DOOR 1931
[Cat. no. 80, p. 96]

39 PETRA IM ROSENHAG 1931
[Cat. no. 83, p. 98]

39 THE QUEEN'S DISH 1932
[Cat. no. 88, p. 100]

40 BRIAR CUP 1932
[Cat. no. 93, p. 101]

41 THE FARM DOOR 1937
[Cat. no. 102, p. 104]

42 APHRODITE IN AULIS 1941
[Cat. no. 110, p. 108]

51 VIEW FROM GATWICK HOUSE, ESSEX, APRIL 1946
[Cat. no. 117, p. 112]

52 FLORA IN CALIX-LIGHT 1950
[Cat. no. 130, p. 119]

53 Y CYFARCHIAD I FAIR (The Greeting to Mary) c. 1963
[Cat. no. 142, p. 126]

54 DVM MEDIVM SILENTIVM 1952
[Cat. no. 151, p. 131]

63 EX DEVINA PVLCHRITVDINE 1956
[Cat. no. 155, p. 133]

64 VERE DIGNVM 1961
[Cat. no. 166, p. 138]

[11]

CHRONOLOGY

1895
1 November: born in Brockley, Kent, son of James Jones, printer's overseer, of Holywell, Flintshire, and Alice Bradshaw, daughter of a mast-and-block maker of Rotherhithe.

1901–2
Earliest surviving drawings, mostly of animals.

1910–14
Attended Camberwell School of Art; taught by A.S. Hartrick. His ambition to become an illustrator of Welsh history or an animal painter.

1915–18
Served on the Western Front with the Royal Welch Fusiliers; most of his trench drawings destroyed.

1919
2 January: 'certificate of transfer to reserve on demobilization'.

1919–21
Studied at Westminster School of Art under Walter Bayes and Bernard Meninsky; Sickert an occasional teacher.

1921
Received into the Roman Catholic Church. Went to live with Eric Gill and his family at Ditchling, becoming a postulant in the Guild of St Joseph and St Dominic. He learnt wood-engraving, and illustrated publications of St Dominic's Press.

1923
Admitted as Tertiary of the Order of St Dominic.

1924
August: Gill moved to Capel-y-ffin, in the valley of the Honddu, north of Abergavenny. Jones, who had become engaged to Gill's second daughter Petra, joined the family at Christmas.

1925
Painted landscapes at Capel and on Caldy Island (Ynys Byr) where he stayed in the Benedictine monastery.
Golden Cockerel Press published *Gulliver's Travels* with his wood-engravings.

1926
Painted watercolours at Brockley, Bristol and Capel.

1927
His engagement broken off. Painted on Caldy, at Brockley and at Portslade near Brighton, where his parents rented a villa on the sea front. Visited Blake Centenary Exhibition. Joined the Society of Wood-Engravers.
Publication of *The Chester Play of the Deluge*, Golden Cockerel Press. Joint exhibition with Eric Gill at St George's Gallery.

1928
His friend Ben Nicholson successfully proposed him for election to The Seven and Five Society; he exhibited with the society until 1933 in the company of Ben and Winifred Nicholson, Henry Moore, Barbara Hepworth, Christopher Wood and John Piper.
Visited Lourdes and Salies-de-Béarn, country associated with Roman Gaul and *Le Chanson de Roland*. After his return he started to write an epic poem of the Great War, *In Parenthesis*.
Gill moved to Pigotts in Buckinghamshire.

CHRONOLOGY

1929
Joint exhibition with Eric Gill at the Goupil Gallery. Coleridge's *The Rime of the Ancient Mariner* with ten engravings on copper published by Douglas Cleverdon. First of several visits to Helen Sutherland's home, Rock Hall, near Alnwick, Northumberland.
Did many drawings of animals at London Zoo.

1930
Eye trouble forced him to give up engraving. Saw Botticelli's 'Birth of Venus' in the exhibition of Italian Art at the Royal Academy. Joint exhibition with Ivon Hitchens at Heal's Mansard Gallery.

1930–2
Painted watercolours at Portslade, Brockley, Pigotts, Caldy and Rock Hall. Also made some informal painted inscriptions.

1932
Impressed by Fouquet in the exhibition of *French Art* at the Royal Academy. 18 August: first draft of *In Parenthesis* completed; soon afterwards a period of very fluent painting brought to an end by a nervous breakdown. His friends in The Seven and Five turned more dogmatically in favour of abstract art.

1934
Crossed the Mediterranean to visit Cairo and Jerusalem: a sea voyage had been recommended to cure his chronic insomnia. In Jerusalem *The Anathemata* and the Roman poems were first conceived.

1935–9
Lived for most of the time within view of the sea in Fort Hotel, Sidmouth, Devon. Drew very little at first, more after 1938.

1937
Publication of *In Parenthesis*, Faber, with support from T. S. Eliot. Death of his mother.

1939–45
Returned to London, where he lived with friends or in lodgings for most of the war. London in the Blitz released new energies: the first drafts of *The Kensington Mass, The Wall, The Dream of Private Clitus* and *The Narrows* were written. His first important inscriptions date from c.1942. 'Aphrodite in Aulis' and his large Arthurian drawings, 'The Four Queens' and 'Guenever', all subsequently acquired by the Tate Gallery.
Gill died in 1940. Jones wrote an increasing number of reviews and essays: *Religion and the Muses* 1941, *The Myth of Arthur* 1942, *Art in Relation to War* 1942–3.

1943
Death of his father.

1946
Stayed with Helen Sutherland, who had moved in 1939 to Cockley Moor in Matterdale, above Ullswater: painted Cumberland landscapes. *In Parenthesis* adapted for radio by Douglas Cleverdon, with Dylan Thomas and Richard Burton in the cast.

1947
'In 1947 I had a return of my 1932 breakdown, only much worse, and had to go to Dr C.M.'s nursing home for treatment, that's how I came to be in Harrow. I was there for six months and made incredibly better. And went to Mr Carlile's house so as to be near the nursing home for a while.' In fact, Northwick Lodge became his home until 1964; here he enjoyed the friendship of the other lodgers – several were masters from Harrow – and found the peace to draw and write.

1947–8
Did many drawings of the trees outside his window, culminating in 'Vexilla Regis' (1947). Also drew, in pencil, crayon and chalk, heads of girls observed at Mass.

1949
David Jones, by Robin Ironside, published in the Penguin Modern Painters series, edited by Kenneth Clark.

c.1950
Watercolours of flowers in a glass chalice.

1952
The *Anathemata*, Faber.

1954–5
Retrospective exhibition at the National Museum of Wales, the Tate Gallery, and Aberystwyth, Swansea and Edinburgh.
During the 1950s he suffered from bouts of depression and ill health; visits to central London became rarer.

1956–61
Made many of his finest painted inscriptions.

1959
Epoch and Artist: Selected Writings, Faber, edited by Harman Grisewood.

1962
Painted 'Trystan ac Essyllt'.

1963–64
'Y Cyfarchiad i Fair' (The Annunciation in a Welsh Hill Setting) his last major drawing.

1964
Moved to Monksdene Residential Hotel, Harrow.

1965
The *Fatigue* printed at Rampant Lions Press, Cambridge, to mark his 70th birthday.

1966
Visited exhibition of Bonnard at Royal Academy: probably the last exhibition he saw.

1967
Agenda: David Jones Special Issue: includes essays by Kenneth Clark, H.S. Ede and Stuart Pigott.

1968
Painted his last inscription – for Kathleen Raine.

1969
Tribune's Visitation, Fulcrum Press.

1970
June: fell, breaking a bone in his hip. Moved to Calvary Nursing Home, where the Little Sisters of Mary looked after him until his death.

1972
Word and Image IV: exhibition at the National Book League, subsequently toured Wales.

1974
The Sleeping Lord and Other Fragments, Faber.
Made a Companion of Honour.
28th October: died at Calvary Nursing Home.
13th December: Solemn Requiem at Westminster Cathedral.

1975
The Kensington Mass, Agenda Editions.
Memorial exhibitions at Kettle's Yard, University of Cambridge and Anthony d'Offay Gallery, London.

1975–6
Forty-two works acquired by public collections.

1976
Exhibitions at the University of Stirling and Manchester Cathedral.

1978
The Dying Gaul and Other Writings, Faber, edited by Harman Grisewood.

CHRONOLOGY

1979
Exhibition shown at Anthony d'Offay Gallery and National Gallery of Modern Art, Edinburgh.

1980
Exhibition of Inscriptions at Anthony d'Offay Gallery.

37 THE WATERFALL, AFON HONDDU FACH 1926

61 JULY CHANGE 1929

THE ART OF DAVID JONES

Matter and spirit — both are real and both good. David Jones's art affirms this truth. 'We should miss all the quality of his work,' his friend Eric Gill observed, 'if we did not see that it is a combination of two enthusiasms, that of the man who is enamoured of the spiritual world and at the same time as much enamoured of the material body in which he must clothe his vision.'[1] To balance body and spirit was not simple for a British artist in the early twentieth century. The ease with which realism could be achieved threatened to empty images of meaning beyond the descriptive. Throughout his life David Jones was afraid, perhaps too afraid, that his painting might lapse into material grossness, but the contemporary escape-routes bypassing the snare of illusionism — egocentric expressionism, or reliance upon abstract values — failed to meet his need. In 1930, Gill was right to assert, in the earliest essay on Jones, 'What concerns him is the universal thing showing through the particular thing, and as a painter it is this showing through that he endeavours to capture. The eye sees particular things, but the man's delight in the physical vision is checked by the mind's apprehension informing it.'[2]

David Jones's earliest drawings tell of the eye's delight in particular things. At seven, he drew with rapt excitement a 'Bear' (Cat. no.24) dancing in the street of his native Brockley. By that young age, he had decided that drawing was the activity he would pursue later in life: 'to attempt to convey on paper this or that object seemed to me as natural a desire as, say, stroking the cat.'[3] The metaphor is apt, for all his life drawing remained a gesture of affection, an act of praise. Fortunately, his parents understood such gestures: his mother had drawn well in her youth; as a printer's overseer, his father was concerned with the appearance of the printed page. But we would be quite wrong to suppose David Jones was brought up in an atmosphere of aestheticism. To the mature poet and artist, it was important that his maternal grandfather, Ebenezer Bradshaw, had been a mast-and-block maker in Rotherhithe, for that ancestry was a lanyard that linked him to ships, to the Pool of London, and to all that pertains to the craft of the ship's carpenter. From the family tradition he learnt respect for craftsmanship, for the right making of things —

we'll fay that hounding trim and proper

He has Eb Bradshaw proclaim in his great poem, published in 1952, The

Anathemata.[4] So to the gesture of affection – the stroking of the cat – was added the understanding that a drawing or painting is more than an imitation, it is a thing made according to the disciplines of a craft.

His mind's apprehension of the universal necessarily matured more slowly. He was brought up in a devout Anglican family. His father, Jonas Jones, came from Holywell in Flintshire and retained the Low Church persuasion of his Welsh parentage. David Jones never forgot his father's readings from Bunyan's *Pilgrim's Progress*. At Camberwell Art School, which he attended between 1909 and 1914, he nursed the ambition to illustrate historical subjects, 'preferably from Welsh history and legend'.[5] But contemporary history burst in upon his juvenile romanticism: in 1915 he enlisted as a private in the Royal Welch Fusiliers. His experience in the trenches deepened his understanding of the Christian doctrine of the Atonement, of sin and redemption. Bunyan's allegory of the conflict of good and evil, Private Jones now apprehended in the Wasteland of the Western Front, and that apprehension became an indelible feature of his mental landscape. In the trenches he became 'inwardly Catholic' and it was there that he first witnessed, through a chink in the wall of a dimly lit byre, a Roman Catholic Mass. In 1919, back in mufti, he was awarded a government grant to study at Westminster School of Art which, by a happy chance, was in Vincent Square, just round the corner from Westminster Cathedral. When he soon formed the habit of slipping out from the life class to attend Mass, a lifelong meditation on the relationship between the activity of the artist and the liturgy of the Church had begun.

As his understanding of the Eucharist deepened, an unexpected analogy presented itself. 'I used to say to chaps that I thought the theory of Post-Impressionism, about a painting and what not being a *thing* and not the impression of something, was analogous to what the Catholic Church maintained in her dogma of the Mass – they thought I was cracked (especially the Catholic ones!)'.[6] Although he later paid tribute to his teachers at the Westminster, in particular to Bernard Meninsky and to Sickert, who occasionally gave classes, he hungered after a broader vision of the role of the artist than the conventional art school could offer. The exhaustion of the academic tradition, the value of which he perceived, left a vacuum which the cult of individual sensibility could not fill. In the current idiom he could not discover for himself the right relation of body and spirit – the universal shining through the particular.

ERIC GILL AND DITCHLING

Lack of understanding at art school led David Jones to look elsewhere. In any case he was by then, in his mid-twenties, a rather elderly student. In

January 1921, he travelled down to Ditchling in Sussex to visit the stone-carver, engraver, and designer of lettering, Eric Gill. Immediately he recognized a master, 'a true master in the sense that Morris was a master'; a dogmatic man, inclined to over-simplify, but one whose advice 'to start again with something that can be done with reasonable certainty – "proceed from the known",'[7] was salutary at that moment in time. That summer Jones returned to stay at Ditchling. In September, he was formally received into the Roman Catholic church. In late November 1921 he went to live with the Gill household.

Leaving the art school in London, Jones joined a craft guild, the Ditchling Guild of St Joseph and St Dominic. This community of Dominican Tertiaries had been founded in 1919 by Hilary Pepler and Eric Gill as 'a religious fraternity for those who make things with their hands'. Exchanging studio for workshop, canvas and brush for chisel and T-square, Jones was set to make looms. This was Gill's way of knocking the aesthetic nonsense out of the art student to lead him 'to start again with something that can be done with reasonable certainty'. According to the testimony of the apprentice, as an attempt to master the carpenter's craft, it was not a success.

Although carpentry was his principal work during the first months at Ditchling, soon after his arrival he was learning to engrave on wood. Etching and lithography, rather than engraving, were the techniques in fashion at art schools in the 1910s, though there is no evidence that Jones was taught either. The Guild of St Joseph and St Dominic was a pioneer in the revival of wood-engraving in England in the 1920s. It appealed to the community for reasons which Gill explained in his introduction to John Beedham's *Wood Engraving*, a little book published by the Guild's own press, St Dominic's, in 1920. 'The advantage of wood-engraving,' Gill wrote, 'is that it does away with several sets of middle men and places responsibility on the shoulders of the workman. The workman who draws, engraves and prints his own blocks is master of the situation . . . Another advantage of wood-engraving is that it forces upon the workman some respect for the thing itself.'[8] David Jones discovered this second advantage. It led him away from the easy descriptive realism which he could achieve thanks to a sharp eye and long art school training. The limitation imposed by the medium of wood-engraving concentrated eye and mind upon essentials. In his earliest prints, such as the 'Madonna and Child', (Cat. no.2), of 1923, the difficulty of the unfamiliar medium enforced simplicity of line and boldness of tonal contrast. In the smallness of scale the engraver has discovered a monumentality which appears as natural as the Giottesque grandeur of Henry Moore's contemporary studies.

In looking at the 'Mocking of Christ', (Cat. no.26), from the Chapel at Ditchling, we might – at least for a moment – mistake it for the work of an untutored painter whereas it is in fact the work of a young man who has abjured his hard-won accomplishment. Ironically, with the passing of the years, the paintings and engravings Jones made at Ditchling appear to be stylistically the most self-conscious of all his works. Their affinity with the Early Christian primitivism of Gill's carvings, such as the Westminster Cathedral Stations of the Cross, is obvious. But echoes sound from further afield. The movements of the soldiers mocking Christ are comparable with those of the manikin figures of Jones's exact contemporary, William Roberts, whose work he very likely saw in the exhibition of erstwhile Vorticists, *Group X*, which was held in London in the spring of 1920. His familiarity with the Continental sources of the style, Fernand Léger for example, we can only surmise. But one passage in *In Parenthesis* shows to what effect he could describe the theatre of war – a night march up to the line – in terms of the syntax of Cubism, not only its dehumanized geometry but also its synthetic, dramatic lighting:

> Sometimes his bobbing shape showed clearly; stiff marionette jerking on the uneven path; at rare intervals he saw the whole platoon, with Mr Jenkins leading.
> Wired dolls sideway inclining, up and down nodding, fantastic troll-steppers in and out the uncertain cool radiance, amazed crook-back miming, where sudden chemical flare, low-flashed between the crazy flats, flood-lit their sack-bodies, hung with rigid properties –
> the drop falls,
> you can only hear their stumbling off, across the dark proscenium.[9]

In this passage the narrative takes on a distant impersonality; the narrator watches the puppet-show from the far side of the proscenium. Then the perspective shifts abruptly to the interior life: 'Half-minds, far away, divergent, own-thought thinking, tucked away unknown thoughts . . .' The physical uniformity of the marching soldiers contrasts with their psychic individuality, 'each his own thought-maze alone treading'. So in Jones's visual art the formality of a conceptual, geometric style must yield to nuances of individuality: matter must accommodate spirit. Within the strong formality of design in his drawing of the daughters of Eric Gill, (Cat. no.27), each head is incisively individual. Irregular shading produces a strange radiance – sign of the vibrance of inner life, each her own thought-maze treading.

The drawing of Elizabeth, Petra, and Joanna Gill gives us a clue that it was not Gill's workshop therapy or Thomist philosophy which released Jones from the crisis which afflicted him at art school so much as the deepening of an emotional life in which religious conviction and personal feeling were dovetailed.

At Ditchling until 1924, and subsequently at Capel-y-ffin, near Abergavenny, and at Pigotts in Buckinghamshire, Jones shared in the life of the Gill family. He became devoted to Eric and his wife Mary, and to their daughters and adopted son. In the first months at Ditchling, he lived in the 'bachelors' quarters' next to the Gill's house, the Crank. The garden, with its brick paths and hen-coop, may be seen in 'The Garden Enclosed' (Cat. no.28). A letter of Gill's of 13 December 1921 affords a glimpse of family life in the evenings: 'Petra is sewing and David Jones is reading *Twelfth Night* to her'. Petra was only fifteen; three years later she and David became engaged to be married. The growth of these emotional ties was interwoven with participation in the religious life of the Guild of St Joseph and St Dominic. In the small chapel next door to the workshops of the Guild, the Office of the Blessed Virgin Mary was recited daily. When, in 1923, Jones became a Tertiary of the Order of St Dominic, he took his turn as cantor. In such a context, analogies between the narratives and mysteries of Holy Scripture and the activities of daily life proposed themselves quite naturally to his imagination. It was no accident that the joint patron of the Guild was St Joseph the Carpenter: the Holy Family were often in their thoughts. Christian names were no mere convention but bright reminders of the saints. For the birthdays and name-days of his closest friends Jones made little drawings of scenes from the lives of the saints; he delighted in the names of his betrothed, Petra, the female form of Peter, and Helen – name of so many associations – wife of Constantine, discoverer of the True Cross, and before that of Trojan fame. When he painted himself embracing Petra in the garden of the Crank, he entitled it 'The Garden Enclosed', in allusion to the Song of Songs iv:12 'A garden inclosed is my sister, my spouse'. The reference to the great love song of the Old Testament is peculiarly appropriate, for in this little painting we can recognize the immanence of the divine in things earthy and familiar – a quality perhaps better known in the works of Stanley Spencer.

In the preface to *The Anathemata*, published in 1952, David Jones wrote: 'It is of no consequence to the shape of the work how the workman came by the bits of material used in making that shape. When the workman is dead the only thing that will matter is the work, objectively considered.'[10] But in spite of the grand impersonality of his poems – the first person singular is almost never used – his works are fired by autobiographical experience. 'For men can but proceed from what they know, nor is it for the mind of this flesh to practise poiesis, *ex nihilo*.'[11] His paintings are autobiographical in the elementary sense that they depict places that he had usually lived in for long spells; more profoundly, in the matter of associations, in the signs he tried and tested for validity, his art, whether an Arthurian illustration (Cat. no.109) or a litany to the universal female protectress he called *The Tutelar of the Place*, sprang from the experience of particular places and particular moments of fellowship and affection. Service on the Western Front was one such experience to which his imagination constantly returned. Family life with the Gills, ordered by a diurnal pattern of worship and of making, shot through with sacred and carnal passion, was another. Within that goodly frame his imagination was harnessed to the contactual and familiar.

WALES — THE BRIGHT HILL-RHYTHMS

In August 1924 Eric Gill and three families, one pony, chickens, cats, dogs, goats, ducks, geese, and two magpies travelled from Ditchling to the Black Mountains, north of Abergavenny. There they were installed — a veritable Noah's ark — high in the valley of the Honddu, in the former monastery at Capel-y-ffin. David Jones joined them at Christmas. It was a homecoming to the land of his fathers. Over the next three years he spent much of his time in Wales, painting in the open at Capel and at Caldy, the island off the coast of Pembrokeshire. The move from the relaxed, ample curves of the Sussex downs (so consonant with Gill's vision), to the irregular inflexions of the Welsh hills and coast, effected a release from the borrowed idiom in which he had been working. In an autobiographical talk he told how he discovered, between 1924 and 1926, a fruitful direction for his work, particularly under 'the impact of the strong hill-rhythms and the bright counter-rhythms of the "afonydd dyfroedd" (water-brooks) which make so much of Wales a "plurabelle".'[12]

There is no stillness in the landscape at Capel. The movement of streams, wind, rain and cloud ceaselessly transforms. 'Within a very short time from the beginning of heavy rain, freshets break out all over the upper slopes of the enclosing mountains, splashes of shining white on the dun background, some remaining as small spurts, others gradually become threads, ribbons, streams of water which indeed seem to be living.'[13] David Jones must have witnessed many times the transformation Donald Attwater describes. Movement, change which reveals the unchanging, transmogrification as he calls it, from 1925 onwards becomes his quarry. Already in 'Tir y Blaenau' (Cat. no.29), which must have been drawn very soon after his arrival at Capel, we can see how his style is losing its hardness. The fitting together to make a shape, the draughtsman's carpentry, no longer relies upon an imposed geometry. Harmony between surface and depth is achieved quite naturally by allowing the contours of the mountains to climb the page, their contours flexed against the margins. That was a gift of a landscape where the mountains press in on every side and the ground falls away at your feet: you couldn't paint a Claude Lorraine in Breconshire, David Jones once remarked.[14] 'Tir y Blaenau' is organized around the distinctive shape of the Tump, the hill rising in the centre of the valley to the north of Capel. From this time onwards nearly all Jones's paintings and engravings are similarly organized around a powerful central shape: it may be the figure of Mary, standing within a cave, as in the dry-point of 1928 (Cat. no. 12), or it may be a bay on Caldy Island (Cat. no. 44). In each case the composition eddies around the centre, and is sustained by interchange between negative and positive shapes. This interchange is the source of the essentially abstract quality of his greatest work. Following any contour in the drawing of 1926, 'Y Twmpa Nant Honddu', (Cat.no.42) one can see that it belongs simultaneously to two shapes – or rather, one is led constantly to reinterpret which side of the line delimits the contained shape and which side is open to the space and air. Such mysterious exchange between solid and void, such 'shape-shifting' illusions, became ever more vital to Jones's imaginative art.

The organization of shapes is not the sole source of unity in 'Tir y Blaenau'. The individual marks of pencil and brush share a distinctive character, irregular yet rhythmic, tremulous yet bold. He has rediscovered the handwriting of sharp jabs, with which, at seven, he drew the 'Bear' at Brockley, and which will become the unmistakable signature of his visual art. Individually these marks may appear graceless, undisciplined, even messy; yet at the right distance they signal across the paper in vibrant patterns. The matrix of white paper is crucial to this essentially linear art; the character of each touch must tell. Jones was never completely at home working in oils. When he did so he favoured a white ground, diluted his paints with turpentine and applied them thinly. In watercolour (and later in chalks) he transforms the whiteness of the page into a source of unity and instead of using the untouched paper to describe the highlights according to a strictly tonal system, as in traditional watercolour technique, he uses whiteness to accentuate the rhythmic play of line.

The formal sophistication of David Jones's visual art deserves careful consideration, and yet the further we move towards the language of formal analysis, the greater the danger that we may miss the springs of his imagination. The rhythmic play of line is never merely arabesque: it stops

and starts at the dictates of feeling, it registers the excitement of things seen
and loved. Rhythm itself proposes to the imagination analogies and connections which reach beyond the visual. Before David Jones had ever published a line of poetry, his sensibility was discovering the 'inward continuity of site', the historic resonance, of the Welsh border landscape.
Already in the Capel drawings of 1924–6, the imagery of his poem, The
Sleeping Lord, written some forty years later, is prefigured:

>   The twisted flax-wick . . .
>   bends one way
>   and the wind-bowed elder boughs
>   and the pliant bending of the wild elm
>   (that serves well the bowyers)
>   and the resistant limbs
>   of the tough, gnarled derwen even
>   lean all to the swaying briary-tangle
>   that shelters low
>   in the deeps of the valley-wood
>   the fragile blodyn-y-gwynt
>   and the wind-gusts do not slacken
>   but buffet stronger and more chill
>   as the dusk deepens
>   over the high gwaundir . . .[15]

The central theme of the poem is the hoped-for return – and yet the
continual presence – of the figure of the redeemer, the once and future
king, whose recumbent body is identified with the configuration of the
land. The landscape of the Black Mountains – the bony contours of the
land, the gnarled limbs of the derwen (oaks) – lent itself to such anthropomorphic analogy.

CITY AND COUNTRY

David Jones's watercolours of 1926–7 show considerable variety of scene
and subject. He painted in the mountains at Capel, by the sea at Caldy
Island in Pembrokeshire, in the town at his parents' home at Brockley, and
by the sea again at Portslade, near Brighton. The longer we contemplate his
watercolours, the stronger our sense that these worlds are not separate. A
subtle interfusion takes place in the artist's mind. The habit of association
is made plain in the verbal imagery of In Parenthesis, where the desolation of
the Front is evoked in terms of a familiar scene closer to home: 'the untidied squalor of the loveless scene spread far horizontally, imaging unnamed discomfort, sordid and deprived as ill-kept hen-runs that back on

68 CATH GARTREF 1930

70 PIGOTTS FARM 1930

79 Place for Ships 1931

80 Manawydan's Glass Door 1931

sidings on wet weekdays where wasteland meets environs and punctured bins ooze canned-meats discarded, tyres to rot, derelict slow-weathered iron-ware disintegrates between factory-end and nettle-bed.'[16] No doubt such unloved margins between city and country were known to Jones from his suburban childhood. What is remarkable is that he was capable of reversing the simile: 'A trench lived in in 1915 might easily "get into" a picture of a back garden in 1925 and by one of those hidden processes, transmogrify it – impart somehow or other, a vitality which otherwise it might not possess.'[17]

Looking at the Brockley watercolours, not of 1925 but of 1926, we can see what David Jones is driving at. The fences of 'A Town Garden', (Cat. no.32), have the air of palisades, defending separate territories, creating that sense of safe enclosure which he knew to be as needful for any Romano-Briton in his hill-fort as for a Tommy in his dug-out. We should be wrong to suppose that the prayer which he addresses to Mary in the *Tutelar of the Place* –

> Sweet Mair devise a mazy-guard
> in and out and round about
> double-dance defences
> countermure and echelon meanders round
> the holy mound
>   fence within the fence
> pile the dun ash for the bright seed . . . [18]

is answered only in the deeps of a valley-wood by Nant Honddu, for he discovers a mazy-guard also in a back garden at Brockley. After the vision of Wales he sees the street where he grew up with new eyes. The serried ranks of houses in 'Suburban Order', (Cat. no.33), jog a memory of infantry parading; and the trees within this regimented pattern grow as signs of living grace. Or one tree may be pollarded, a lone memorial of the lopped and splintered trees of No-Man's Land. No rubicon runs here to separate the observed from the imaginative: the great sign-bearing tree of 'Vexilla Regis', (Cat. no.122), will grow from roots in a town-child's garden.

SEA-CHANGE

Though the roofs might gleam on wet weekdays, one element was missing in the view from Brockley – water. The waterfalls (Cat. no.37), the freshets, the streams at Capel, ran swift and clear. In David Jones's eyes, their water was the water of the Sacrament of Baptism, one of the primary *signa* of Christ. Painting all day on the cliffs at Caldy, he watched the changing of the tide and the catspaws moving over the face of the sea.

Many years later he wrote, 'The sea has had quite a *big* influence, I believe, on my stuff, though it's not been noted as an ingredient – whereas the hills and flowers etc have.'[19] That this should not have been noted is surprising, for surely it is clear that the movement of waves, the jagged rocks of the Pembrokeshire coastline – so rich in geological faulting – and above all the shimmering light of the sea, contributed as much as the hill-rhythms to the loosening of his style.

'Tenby from Caldy Island', (Cat. no.31), of 1925, and the Brockley watercolours of 1926, are drawn with hard-edged differentiation of planes in an idiom which derives ultimately from Cézanne. The schematic shading and the shorthand simplifications of foliage, point to Jones's familiarity with the contemporary paintings of Paul Nash. Wood-engraving was suited to this conceptual approach to form. Since every line engraved on the block prints white, line is wedded to light. In the engraving of the 'Whale' from the Book of Jonah, (Cat. no.7), of 1926, the luminosity of the engraved lines is beautifully gauged. Jones has noted (perhaps while he was staying at Caldy in 1925) how the sea tends to produce a radiant *contre-jour*, throwing shapes into silhouette. Light no longer shines *upon* but shines *through*, rendering the visual field translucent.

From January to March 1927, David Jones stayed once again with the Benedictine monks on Caldy Island. If it was too cold or too windy to paint in the open, he worked in the scriptorium of the monastery. There, very likely, he engraved the blocks of the *Chester Play of the Deluge*, which was published by the Golden Cockerell Press later that year. In the ninth engraving, the 'Dove' (Cat. no.10), the shape-shifting translucency reveals – as through a glass darkly – the mountains beneath the face of the receding waters. The quality of contour we noted in the landscapes of Capel, ambiguity as to which side of a line delimits a contained shape and which side is open to the space and air, is now controlled to sublime effect. The schematism of the Book of Jonah is transformed by a new fineness and irregularity in the individual marks of the graver: the handwriting which was becoming such a pervasive source of unity in his watercolours is now evident in his engravings also.

'Rocks and Surf, Caldy' (Cat. no. 44) is recognizably contemporary with, the 'Dove'. The neat cross-hatching in pencil on the clouds is an engraver's device and one much favoured by Paul Nash. The linear, wayward play of the tip of the brush is unlike anything in Nash; it is utterly personal and yet looks back, instinctively, to a British tradition. Stylistically, 'Rocks and Surf' might be described as an attempt to reconcile Hogarth and Cézanne – the eighteenth century play of line, and the Post-Impressionist grasp of form. Jones had realized at Westminster Art School that the Post-Impressionist aesthetic, 'about painting ... being a *thing* and not the impression of something' accorded with his own inclinations. From Cézanne more than any other modern master he learnt how form and space reciprocally interlock. And yet he was responsive to other modes of vision hardly deemed fashionable by Bloomsbury critics. In eighteenth-century British painting he responded to a certain freedom of brushwork expressive of character. He admired it in Gainsborough when a vital balance is struck between flowing strokes and staccato jabs of the brush. In Julius Caesar Ibbetson's paintings of Wales, where the little groups of figures are so much at one with the tumbling rhythm of the landscape, he recognized a true feeling for locality. He also enjoyed Richard Wilson's views of Wales, recapturing in his own something of the grandeur of Wilson's bowls of space. Above all, it was William Hogarth's 'beauty of a composed intricacy of form', his serpentine line, which was to lead Jones away from the anglicised versions of Cézanne towards a personal vision and one more in keeping with the shores and hills in which he found himself.

THE SEVEN AND FIVE SOCIETY

At this point it may be as well to turn away from a strictly chronological approach to consider more broadly Jones's relationship to contemporary art between the mid-1920s and 1932. The first point to note is that David Jones never became dominated by Eric Gill. Unlike other members of the Ditchling group he had some seven years of art school training behind him. He had enjoyed the teaching of Walter Sickert, in his view the greatest English painter since Turner. Bernard Meninsky, whose life class he attended at the Westminster, exhibited with the Vorticists. Such metropolitan contacts were not entirely severed. However long Jones stayed at Capel and at Caldy, his parents' house at Brockley remained his home to which he would return for long spells. 'The Engraver's Workshop', (Cat. no. 57) shows his bedroom there, where he printed many of his engravings, painted still-lifes on the table or views through the window. From this base he could reach the galleries and exhibitions of London; or, from the late 1920s, he would move closer in, staying with his friend Tom Burns in Chelsea. This lifeline to the capital became increasingly important during these years, for there is no doubt that Jones at this time was alert and responsive to contemporary developments in painting.

In England in the 1920s there were two principal groupings of artists. One, the London Group, became bogged down in a new academicism, producing work unkindly described as 'Cézanne mixed with rice pudding'. The other group consisted of painters and sculptors who were sooner or later to join the Seven and Five Society. Founded in 1919, by the late 1920s the Seven and Five had attracted most of the young artists who were to dominate British art over the next ten years. David Jones remembered the exhibitions as the gayest and most varied in London; the mood was adventurous and undoctrinaire. 'The line of the Seven and Five is, I think,' Jim Ede wrote in his preface to the seventh exhibition in January 1927, 'to break quite clearly from the representational in its photographic sense, though not like the Cubists to abandon known shapes. It is to use the everyday objects, but with such a swing and flow that they become living things, they fall into rhythm in the same sort of way that music does, but their vitality comes through colour and form instead of sound and time. They are not so much pictures as ideas settled for the moment on canvas, but ever ready to take flight into some new life.' Ede's words echo Nicholson's thoughts, and it was Nicholson who, in 1928, successfully proposed Jones for membership. He joined a distinguished company, which included Ivon Hitchens, Christopher Wood, Cedric Morris, and Ben and Winifred Nicholson. Frances Hodgkins was elected in 1929; Barbara Hepworth and Henry Moore in 1931. Jones exhibited with the Seven and Five every year until 1933, a five year span which marks a peak in his artistic career and was certainly the period in which he was most closely in touch with the Modern Movement. From Ben Nicholson and Christopher Wood he heard first-hand reports of Picasso's latest work; at the Hampstead home of Jim Ede he met Georges Braque.

In the mid-1920s Ben and Winifred Nicholson and Christopher Wood painted landscape and still-life with childlike simplicity of composition and purity of tone. Like Gill and his Ditchling associates, they were determined to avoid the slickness of representational art: unlike Gill, they avoided the trap of falling back upon earlier stylistic conventions. Their primitivism sprang from directness of vision, an ability to treat everyday objects 'with such a swing and flow that they become living things'. Painting Breton women dancing between the rough walls of their village – white bonnets, white stones, ringed together – Christopher Wood revealed through colour and tone the harmony of person and place. When Winifred Nicholson painted 'Cyclamen' in 1921 (Kettle's Yard, University of Cambridge) she built a painting from a few arresting and intense colours, laid on in unbroken patches and set off by freshest white. Agreeing to a comment by Saunders Lewis that Winifred Nicholson painted not the flowers but 'her wonder', David Jones wrote (in 1971): 'Perhaps we can say, by analogy, that she showed forth the "substance" rather than the "accidents" shining through the apportioned parts of matter that Aquinas said constituted "beauty", and this is exemplified in Winifred's best wonder-making, though the title might be "Flowers in a pot" or what not. I think her most "wonder-making" painting was done in the late 1920s or early '30s when Ben was in his, for want of a better word, "quasi-abstract" phase.'[20]

BEN NICHOLSON

The most liberating of all his associates in the Seven and Five was Ben Nicholson. The two artists shared an instinctive love of lucid whiteness. The whiteness of sea-foam, of Aphrodite born from the sea, of spread altar-cloths, and of a lime-white bangor, are but some of the images of immaculate whiteness to which Jones so often turned in his poetry. Whiteness as a property of things seen, yet a universal quality, a sign: such whiteness was to be distilled in Ben Nicholson's reliefs — and later between the coloured letters of David Jones's painted inscriptions. Already Nicholson's 'Apples and Pears' of 1927 (Kettle's Yard) are suspended in reflected light; parings of green float upon an off-white ground, anchored only by the dark stalks; the cast shadows assume substance and stirring life as the angle of their fall, their length and depth, is varied. Space is created by the juxtaposition of colour and outline, rather than by perspective.

Jones's 'Table Top' (Cat. no.56) of 1928 shows how appreciative he was of Nicholson's tightrope balancing of representation and design. He creates the same yielding, non-perspective space by choosing a high viewpoint and aligning the sides of the table with the margins of his page. Those same edges are marked with a dark, slightly irregular, outline which further accentuates the surface design. This is true also of the sharply pencilled outlines of the simple shapes of the jug and bowls: we are reminded of the bold linearity of engraving on copper which he had practised since 1926, but also, unmistakably, of Nicholson's graphic style. These outlines do not accommodate highlight and shadow, they run unbroken, delineating each shape in its integrity. The intervals between forms stand forth with lovely clarity. Yet whatever the purity of design, we respond also to beauty of light and atmosphere — a quality of representation. As in Nicholson's work, chiaroscuro has been set free of its traditional modelling function. Neither highlights nor shadows are localised. Individual highlights are replaced by a diffused luminosity from the paper which serves as ground. The shadows are free to detach themselves from the objects that cast them, and as in Nicholson, they are often more emphatic in colour and more painterly in handling than the objects themselves. Thus the jug and bowls cast shadows of a positive mid-blue on the tabletop (very like the blue Nicholson admired in Piero della Francesca).

These cast shadows blend imperceptibly with a more generalized 'air shadow' which floats, semi-transparent, over the white paper. Though it frequently overlaps the delineated objects, it is distinguishable from them by the wayward irregularity of the brushwork – evidently executed at speed – which is reinforced here and there by zigzags and spirals in pencil. The colour of these 'air shadows' is a constantly shifting mixture, which may hint at local colour in the wall or floor, but always retains its spatial ambiguity. Finally the picture is pulled together by the strategic deployment of dark accents – which may be read as local colours, or shadows or neither – to be found in the pods of flowers, the deep grey tone within the bowl on the right, the crimson stem in the jug, and the crimson and black outline of the table-leg on the left.

In their oil paintings the Nicholsons and Christopher Wood made a point of not disguising the nature of their materials: the grain of canvas or board is conspicuous, the tracks of the bristle brush show in the oil paint. To follow the promptings of the raw materials, their texture, shape and colour, was one prophylactic against the slickness of representational painting. When, on a visit to St Ives in 1928, they stumbled upon Alfred Wallis painting scrap pieces of cardboard, they recognized a kindred spirit. When two of the Cornishman's pictures were shown at the Seven and Five exhibition the following year, David Jones also recognized something he himself had been feeling his way towards. In later years, several of Wallis's ships sailed dark against a foaming sea of white paint on the walls of Jones's room at Harrow.

Given the example of so many of his associates, why did Jones remain so attached to that least material of all media, watercolour? At Westminster art school, he had approved the Post-Impressionist aesthetic about painting being a thing and not the impression of something; later he saw that view broadened and given workmanlike exposition by Eric Gill; now in the late twenties his contemporaries in the Seven and Five were stressing the material nature of the work of art as an object. Yet his pictures were to be more than paper and paint. He cared deeply for the visible world and all its associations, visible to the eye of the mind. We glimpse the excitement and the struggle in a letter from Caldy: 'There is also a superb plantation of new trees here, which is thrilling, very thrilling – like the Garden of Gethsemane and the Garden of the Tomb and the Garden of – well – the other sort of garden, where Venus disports herself. In fact it is, as 'B' (Belloc) would say, "a garden universal, a garden Catholic" – not that it is a flower garden, but a garden of small trees and winding paths – but oh!

TRUTH TO MATERIA

so difficult to seize hold of when one tries to draw it. I have nearly been demented trying to capture its beauty even but vaguely – I have made four or five furtive attempts.'[21] How were such attempts to be reconciled with the work of art as an object? Undoubtedly there was tension here, which was not eased until he turned to making painted inscriptions – these were to be his answer to the abstract works of his contemporaries in the 1930s, but with meaning and association intact.

Few of David Jones's watercolours are painted without some addition of bodycolour – usually white gouache – to give substance to his paint. By this means he succeeded, with remarkable skill, in achieving effects of brushwork and texture comparable to those that Ben and Winifred Nicholson and Christopher Wood demonstrated in oil. This is evident in the 'Table-top' and more noticeably in 'Roman Land' (Cat. no.54), also of 1928, where nearly all the colours have been rendered opaque by the addition of white; in 'Lourdes' (Cat. no.51) he carried this further by painting entirely in gouache. From this time onwards, when he supervised the framing of his paintings on paper, he framed them as though they were oils by omitting the window-mount which normally separates a watercolour from its frame. Several of his original white frames can be seen in this exhibition. Essentially, they are intended to assert – very much in the manner of Ben Nicholson – that the work of art is an object integral with its frame, rather than the illusion of something viewed through the window of a mount. His instinctive tendency to work with, rather than against, the flatness of his paper (receding lines rhymed with verticals upon the surface) contributed to this effect.

THE ANTIQUITY OF WATERCOLOUR

To seek a deeper understanding of the peculiar blend of watercolour and bodycolour in which Jones discovered true mastery, we must trace him back to Camberwell School of Arts and Crafts in the years before the First World War. It was there that he was taught painting and drawing from the costumed model by A. S. Hartrick, a man he was to remember with affection and gratitude for the rest of his life. A. S. Hartrick (1864–1950), student at the Slade, acquaintance of Van Gogh and Gauguin, is little known now, though the discerning may seek out his drawings of country characters in the British Museum and his studies of English mediaeval stained glass in the Victoria and Albert. Conditioned by the high road surveys of Modernism, we are taken aback to discover an artist who excelled in the best tradition of Victorian graphic illustration, who understood the colour theories of the Post-Impressionists, and who discoursed with feeling on the Wilton Diptych. We can form some idea of his teaching from his two books, *Drawing*, published in 1921, and his autobiography, *A Painter's Pilgrimage*, of 1939. Both testify to Hartrick's belief in drawing as the fundamental artistic discipline. What is remarkable is the range of examples which he drew upon for the education of his pupils. After mentioning the watercolours from tombs in Egypt and China, and the techniques of the Chinese, the Japanese and the Persians, he reminds those who believe that the history of watercolour begins with the English eighteenth century school:

> We had a school of illuminators from the eighth and ninth centuries A.D., beginning with the *Book of Kells* and the *Lindisfarne Gospels*, who understood the use of watercolour for their own purpose in a way that shows they were already supreme craftsmen in the medium ... I have learnt much from a study of the *Luttrell Psalter* and other mediaeval manuscripts, such as "La Bible en images" belonging to the Earl of Leicester, with a picture of the Flood and the raven returning to the ark, as original in design and as supernatural in colour as a nativity by El Greco ... The question of the use of body-colour seems to me to have been settled by the mediaeval illuminators from the thirteenth century, I fancy because they found it goes better with gold ... After these, we find development in the use of the medium in the surprisingly modern-looking landscapes of Albrecht Dürer, which are mostly dependent upon transparent washes, as well as in gouache (miniature) portraits by Holbein, Hilliard and the Clouets ... I believe the above facts bear witness: that in figure painting in watercolour it is necessary to use gouache (i.e. body-colour) or else a pen line in order to keep the necessary control of form to suggest solidity.[22]

I cite this passage at length since it points unerringly to the tradition – far older than that of oil painting – to which David Jones's watercolours belong. The artists Hartrick mentions are all ones that his pupil responded to with enthusiasm; in all their works drawing is not merely preparatory, but a pervasive influence upon the finished painting.

The tradition admired by Hartrick and David Jones began to be submerged in the sixteenth century. It was then that Vasari's distinction between *disegno* and *colore* introduced into the academies of art a divorce between two phases of the creative process, drawing and painting, a split that was confirmed by the enthronement of oil painting as queen of pictorial media. After Vasari, in general, drawing was regarded as preparatory to painting – the working out of a design and the study of its constituent parts – rather than integral to it. This was the norm accepted by Sickert

83 Petra im Rosenhag 1931

88 The Queen's Dish 1932

93 BRIAR CUP 1932

102 THE FARM DOOR 1937

110 Aphrodite in Aulis 1941

when he taught David Jones, whereas Hartrick realized that the separation had only existed in the West, and there only for four hundred years, a short span in the history of man's visual art. Of course, in the nineteenth century many painters had already turned their back on the academic method by painting directly onto their canvases without preliminary drawings, but with hindsight it looks as though Impressionism, the triumph of *colore*, was the ultimate development of the Vasarian distinction. Not surprisingly, the reaction that followed stressed *disegno* and turned to models from before the High Renaissance, or from outside the Western tradition of oil painting, in which the demarcation between drawing and painting, design and colour, was less distinct. Thus, as aids to teaching, Hartrick believed 'in setting up in a conspicuous place an isolated photograph or reproduction of some really choice work of art, such as a drawing by Holbein or one of the Italian masters, an engraving by Dürer, a Sicilian damask pattern, or one from a Greek vase, a piece of fine needlework, a Japanese print.'[23] The young Jones would have studied such exemplars of linear design – notice that none is an oil painting – at Camberwell School of Art. Though at the Westminster, and at Ditchling, Hartrick's lessons were overlaid by other influences, by the late 1920s they were bearing fruit.

It was no accident that his work drew close to that of Ben Nicholson. Both allowed the drawn line to tell in their paintings; both sometimes drew over the top of paint (this is evident in 'Roman Land'); and both valued the grey colour of pencil. By its very nature drawing is further removed from illusionism than oil painting with its full range of colour and tones. Drawing therefore relies to a greater degree upon conventions, that is signs or equivalents for reality. By allowing the drawn line – and lines drawn with the brush – to tell in their finished oils and watercolours, Nicholson and Jones introduced into painting a degree of abstraction which properly belongs to the graphic medium. Nicholson was certainly aware that this was a common feature of European avant-garde painting: Jones knew that he was heir to a British tradition that reached back through Blake to the mediaeval illuminators.

FRANCE – 1928

In the spring of 1928 David Jones travelled to the south of France to stay with the Gills at Salies-de-Béarn. In May he moved on to join Philip Hagreen at the Chalet St Vincent near Lourdes. It is customary to note how this journey took him to a region of historic associations – Roman Gaul and the land of the Chanson de Roland. But it was also the country of 'my paragon Bonnard' and I do not think it is fanciful to see in the large number of watercolours he painted in France a new gaiety, a Gallic fluency. Most of the watercolours, such as 'River Gave' and 'Montes et Omnes Colles' (Cat. nos. 52, 53) were evidently painted at speed; the shadows, instead of being darker than the lights, are conjured, as in Bonnard, by contrasts of colour; the darks, freed from marking the shaded facets of objects, condense into small flecks and blobs, which enliven the paler washes with their staccato rhythm. At first glance we may be reminded of Raoul Dufy; looking closer we recognize a tenderness quite unlike Dufy's bravura. The tall, slender branches bending to the wind, the reflections in the fast-flowing Gave, and the tumbling contours of the hills are described with such gentleness that observed particulars take on the mystery of revelation. Far from generalizing, the track of David Jones's brush is constantly varied; thin washes alternate with drily brushed strokes of thicker paint, which are often intense and unexpected in colour – orange and blue light up the foliage. This handwriting we have met before, but from 1928 onwards it becomes ever more pervasive. At the same time, as can be observed in 'Roman Land', the technique of his paintings on paper moves away from the contemporary practice of watercolour to achieve images of painterly *action*, replete with the revisions, the scumbles and the translucencies normally associated with oil painting. It was a technique of working and reworking (without ever quite obliterating) which was to be close to that of his writing. Much later, in 1952, he explained to Desmond Chute:

> My 'method' is merely to arse around with such words as are available to me until the passage in question takes on something of the shape I think it requires and evokes the image I want. I find, or think I find, the process almost identical to what one tries to do in paintin' and drawin'. Having tried, to the best of one's powers, to make the lines, smudges, colours, opacities, translucencies, tightnesses, hardnesses, pencil marks, paint marks, chalk marks, spit-marks, thumb marks, etc. evoke the image one requires as much as poss. one only *hopes* that some other chap, someone looking at the picture *may* recognize the image intended.[24]

In 1928, the year in which he started 'to make the shape with words' published as *In Parenthesis*, this procedure – so unlike the good workmanship approved by Eric Gill – was just beginning to become David Jones's natural habit.

In 1927 Douglas Cleverdon had the brilliant idea of asking David Jones to illustrate Coleridge's *Rime of the Ancient Mariner*. Instead of choosing wood-

THE ANCIENT MARINER

engraving they decided that the eight plates and two vignettes should be engraved on copper. Since Jones was relatively inexperienced in engraving on copper and since corrections were difficult, he made, by his own account, between 150 and 200 pencil drawings for the ten engravings, a labour that occupied him before and after his trip to France in 1928. In an introduction to the *Rime*, only published in 1972, he described his technique:

> I decided that simple incised lines reinforced here and there and as sparingly as possible by cross-hatched areas (e.g. the hull, masts, yards and spars of the stricken ship in the third full-page illustration), was the only way open to me. I decided also that these essentially linear designs should have an undertone over the whole area of the plate, partly as an aid to unification. This is easily and naturally achieved in copper-plate printing by not wiping the plate totally clean of ink before putting it in the press.... the designs were made with that in view, and fall to pieces if printed without it.[25]

After describing the arduousness of the medium and the simplicity it enforced upon him, he continued:

> Although the great masters and superbly skilled craftsmen have performed miracles of accomplished ingenuity in this medium ... yet I am of the opinion that the most specific beauty, that which belongs to copper-engraving, *sui generis*, is a lyricism inherent in the clean, furrowed free, fluent engraved line, as quintessentially linear as the painted lines on one type of Greek vase, or in Botticelli's (strangely neglected) illustrations to the *Divina Commedia* or the purely linear designs in Anglo-Saxon illustrated Mss.[26]

There can be little doubt that illustrating the *Ancient Mariner* sharpened David Jones's vision of the relationship between form and meaning. He recognized that the surface ease of Coleridge's ballad-form 'conceals or discloses deeps and strata of meaning where, in the words of the Psalmist, *Abyssus abyssum invocat*'.[27] Any cleverness or complexity on the engraver's part would be false to the simplicity of the *Rime* and belie the narrator's voice. So Jones's inexperience in copper-engraving and the difficulty of the medium was in some measure an advantage since it precluded realism. But it was the stylistic examples to which, by temperament, he was attracted – Botticelli and his late fifteenth century contemporaries – that showed how a balance might be struck between the firmness of 'a good bodily image' and an immaterial transparency. At Camberwell Hartrick had maintained that Legros' 'method of teaching drawing, based on that of the old Italian Masters, to draw with the point and by the character of the contour rather than the mass in tone, is the best if not the *only* one for the proper training of the student.'[28] Now in the plates to the *Ancient Mariner* (Cat. no. 13), this supple drawing with the contour – so Botticellian in its inflexion – is set off by short parallel hatchings, like those of the Florentine fine manner. In the second plate, the 'Albatross', these hatched shadows do not insist upon the substantiality of bodies but, floating over the surface, describe the wind and space of the sea. Just as Coleridge did not intend his *Rime* to be read as a purely naturalistic account of a voyage and accordingly chose an unsophisticated verse form, so Jones employed the abstraction inherent in the simplicity of line to disclose deeps and strata of meaning, a world of signs. By engraving the Albatross impaled by the Mariner's arrow to the cross-bar of the mast, he likens the shooting of the immaculate bird to the sacrifice of Christ on the Cross. This rather personal interpretation introduces us to a cornerstone of Jones's imagination.

KEEL, RAM AND STAUROS

As the grandson of a ship's carpenter, it was fitting that David Jones should take to his heart the image of the Church as the ship, the Barque of Christ. In its principal timbers, keel and mast, he perceived the salvific wood of Christ's Cross. Over a lifetime of meditation this image unlocked his understanding of the Christian theology of Redemption and its central mystery, the re-enactment of Christ's Passion in the sacrifice of the Mass. 'What is pleaded in the Mass is precisely the argosy or voyage of the Redeemer, his entire sufferings, death, resurrection and ascension. It is this that is offered on behalf of us argonauts and the whole argosy of mankind and indeed in some sense of all earthly creation, which, as Paul says, suffers a common travail.'[29] So it is not only the ship, its keel and mast, but the voyage and we the argonauts who are comprehended within this imagery. I believe a clue is buried here as to why for Jones 'the supposed words of Galileo *Eppur si muove!* apply to any decent painting, however static the content.'[30] Just as the voyage is a metaphor for the journey of the soul, so movement is life itself.

In 1929, the year after Cleverdon published *The Ancient Mariner*, David Jones painted 'The Terrace' (Cat. no. 60). This can be viewed as a picture of things in which we enjoy an essential goodness, the light and breeze of the sea. So dazzling is the light streaming from the sea that it almost obliterates the hard edges of forms. And the breeze reaches the innermost corner of the terrace, stirring the curtains and lifting the edges of the cloth that is held upon the table by the tall vase of flowers. As so often in Jones's mature work, the balance of hues – pale red, cool blue and lemon yellow – create an exhilarating sense of temperature, a visual equivalent for the warmth of the sun and the chill of the breeze.

Far more than in 'Rocks and Surf' of 1927, light has now become the source of life. It is not the still, steady light of Corot or Whistler, but the dynamic light of Turner, the light that flashes in the poems of Gerard Manley Hopkins. David Jones never had a studio, he never sought out the unchanging north light, but preferred to work looking out from a window or a verandah, where the light flooded into his face. In such situations of back-lighting, academic tonal relationships are confounded: an object in the distance silhouetted against a bright light – a steamer against the sea – may appear darker than anything closer to the eye. Where there is much reflected light, as there appears to be in 'The Terrace', objects may not appear faceted by light and shadow. In such confusion of light, David Jones discovers an order of things loved.

If a children's story and Coleridge's *Rime* admit no distinction between the observed and the imaginative, neither can such a distinction be allowed in David Jones's watercolours. By comparison with his later work, his watercolours of the 1920s may seem to be descriptions of the motif relatively free of symbolic association, yet could it be that in the timbers, uprights and transoms of the terrace at Portslade, he discerned the Rootless Tree, the sign of our salvation? The allusion to the salvific wood is not as explicit as in the Ancient Mariner's mast and cross-bar, but the sense of voyage is more pervasively present – less in the imagery of ships, than in the turbulent narrative of the brushmarks themselves. Just as the axle-tree stands at the still centre of the turning world – *stat crux dum volvitur orbis* – so the curiously branched uprights supporting the transom are set against the restless sea. The motif discloses its meaning to an imaginative mind. There is no code to be broken, no veil to be drawn, only the discovery to be made of stillness in movement.

CELTIC SURREALISM

If the 'Terrace' is compared with a watercolour painted in the same house at Portslade two years later, 'Manawydan's Glass Door' (Cat. no. 80), it appears that the essentials of Jones's style have changed little, though there is a new fluency and assurance in the brushwork. However, this similarity disguises a shift that has taken place in the painter's attitude to observed motifs. The 'Terrace' belongs to that category of window views that were so popular with French and then with English painters in the 1920s: the works of Matisse and Bonnard, and Ben and Winifred

Nicholson spring to mind. At first, the window was primarily a formal device that offered the painter a strong compositional frame and allowed the juxtaposition of foreground and distance without a complete loss of spatial logic. Both David Jones and Ben Nicholson could give the same sense of immediacy to a jug on a sill as to a boat in a bay or a pony in a field without denying their separation in space. By 1930 such juxtapositions had become in the work of both Ben Nicholson and Paul Nash more deliberately metamorphic. The exhibition of Giorgio de Chirico at Tooth's in 1928 had brought a whiff of Surrealism to London. While Nicholson set out by a new route to re-explore the elusive territory of Cubist space, Nash was attracted by Surrealism's power to bare the mystery of natural forms. 'Manawydan's Glass Door' is an utterly personal picture and yet it is closer to the preoccupations of the artistic avant-garde than has been recognized: just as Nash's harbour (c.f. 'Harbour and Room' 1932–6, Tate Gallery) invades the interior of a room, so Jones's sea flows through the glass door. This is the surrealism of the Celtic wonder-tales – the flowered carpet is transformed by a spell into the seashore starred with anenome.

We find authority for such interpretation in the artistic autobiography David Jones wrote in 1935, the year before the International Surrealist Exhibition came to London. The last paragraph, quoted below, was not written by an antiquarian escapist but by an artist who had pondered with rare historical breadth of imagination the very topical problem of the relationship between illusion and reality, image and meaning:

> I should like to speak of a quality which I rather associate with the folk-tales of Welsh or Celtic derivation, a quality congenial and significant to me which in some oblique way has some connection with what I want in painting. I find it impossible to define, but it has to do with a certain affection for the intimate creatureliness of things – a care for, and appreciation of the particular genius of places, men, trees, animals, and yet withal a pervading sense of metamorphosis and mutability. That trees are men walking. That words 'bind and loose material things'. I think Carroll's Alice Books and the Hunting of the Snark inherit, through what channel I do not know, something akin to this particular quality of the Celtic tales. The Snark is always a Boojum in the Celtic legend, and tragically so in much Celtic history. The Hunting of the Snark has for me an affinity to the Gododin of Aneurin and the Hunting of the Boar Trwyth in the Olwen tale, and the Grail Quest also. Interestingly enough, the English folk-song commencing

'There were three jovial Welshmen' seems to pay tribute to this thing. In any typical English hunting song the huntsmen meet to hunt the fox, they hunt a fox and they kill a fox. But the three jovial Welshmen meet to hunt a mortal creature, but at the 'view' the thing hunted turns out to be a 'ship a-sailing', which turns out to be the moon, which turns out to be made of cheese – I forget the sequence, and the detail, but it is interesting in this connection.[31]

It would be misleading to suppose that David Jones's enjoyment of the metamorphic owed very much to contemporary movements in art. When as a young child he used to pay his sister a penny to read to him the book he most liked hearing read was the story of King Arthur's knights in a series called *Books for the Bairns*.[32] Though the ambition, nursed at Camberwell, to be an illustrator of Welsh history and legend had seemingly been laid aside, yet his imagination still fed upon such things. On 30 May 1925 he inscribed 'Read 2nd time' in W. Lewis Jones's *King Arthur in History and Legend*.[33] His imaginative response to Malory's *Morte Darthur* and to the early Welsh stories collectively known as the *Mabinogion* gave to *In Parenthesis*, the writing of which stretched from 1928 to 1933, a mythic dimension comparable to that of Eliot's *Wasteland* and Joyce's *Ulysses*. Strangely, in the twenties access to the tradition which gave to the words of Eliot and Joyce such resonance of meaning seemed to be denied to visual artists by influential critics such as Clive Bell. By 1930 the dominant mode of contemporary painting was less inhospitable to the quality Jones admired in Celtic folk-tales. The naive vision exemplified by Wallis and admired by members of the Seven and Five played a part in this relaxation of attitudes; the influence of Surrealism, though hardly strong in England at first, would at least have allowed David Jones a greater licence in the treatment of his subjects.

THE MOTHER AND BRIDE

Such licence did not, however, weaken the critical ban on literary subjects being treated in painting. Not surprisingly, it was in engraving that Jones had first tried his hand at overtly Arthurian subjects. Douglas Cleverdon had hoped that *The Ancient Mariner* might be followed by a complete *Morte Darthur*. The one specimen dry-point, 'Wounded Knight', (Cat. no.15), which David Jones engraved before illness scotched the project, shows what a personal vision he brought to the illustrator's task. Arthur, mortally wounded in the Battle of Camlann, lies in the lap of the goddess, Arianrhod: a Celtic *pietà* which reminds us that the perennial power of the Arthurian stories lies in their re-enactment of the redemption drama of Christian sacrifice in the familiar terrain of Britain.

In the preface to In Parenthesis, Jones wrote, 'For the old authors . . . the embrace of battle seemed one with the embrace of lovers.'³⁴ The interweaving of sexual love, battle, and spiritual quest which runs through the Arthurian stories is announced in the 'Wounded Knight' and developed with far greater complexity in 'Aphrodite in Aulis' (Cat. no.110) of 1941 (see pp.60–62). In the same year as the Wounded Knight', 1930, he made his most beautiful wood-engraving, 'The Bride' (Cat. no.16). Described in a note to The Anathemata as 'both bride and mother of the cult-hero,' the Virgin Mary is shown here placing a votive candle at the feet of the Crucifix. So, under a different aspect, the same mystery is celebrated as in the 'Wounded Knight'. The Bride calls in the spirit of the Song of Songs (ii:9):

My beloved is like a roe or a young hart:
behold he standeth behind our wall,
he looketh forth at the windows,
shewing himself at the lattice.

In January of the year David Jones engraved 'The Bride' he was best man at the marriage of his former betrothed, Petra Gill, to Denis Tegetmeier. The following year he painted a portrait of Petra, entitling it 'Petra im Rosenhag' (Cat. no. 83), alluding to Renaissance paintings of the Madonna in a rose arbour. In the watercolour, a Georgian candlestick has taken the place of the hearse or harrow on which the Bride impaled her votive light. The candles and flowers indicate we are still in the presence of a shrine. So, with the title in mind, we may be prompted to perceive in the particular beauty of this mother a reflection of the beauty of She who bore the Incarnate Logos.

In October 1929, Jones wrote to Jim Ede, 'I'm reading a very interesting book about the Grail legend – very *Golden Boughish* but I think, in the main, sound, by a woman called Jessie Weston.'³⁵ This exploration of the archetype of the Grail legends, mined to such effect by Eliot in The Wasteland, was closely annotated by Jones. The result was his own modest version of the Wasteland, the wood engraving of 1931, entitled 'He Frees the Waters' (Cat. no. 17). It seems that this was conceived as an independent engraving, though later it served, very appropriately, as an illustration to The Anathemata. In addition to its haunting beauty, the engraving of the unicorn, who frees the waters and so fructifies the wasted land, introduces us to imagery more elusively present in a number of watercolours of 1931–2 and circa 1950. Below the unicorn a chalice stands upon what is probably a ruckled cloth – the corporal of the altar. Two of the instruments of

117 VIEW FROM GATWICK HOUSE, ESSEX, APRIL 1946

130 FLORA IN CALIX-LIGHT 1950

142 Y Cyfarchiad i Fair (The Greeting to Mary) c.1963

THE ART OF DAVID JONES

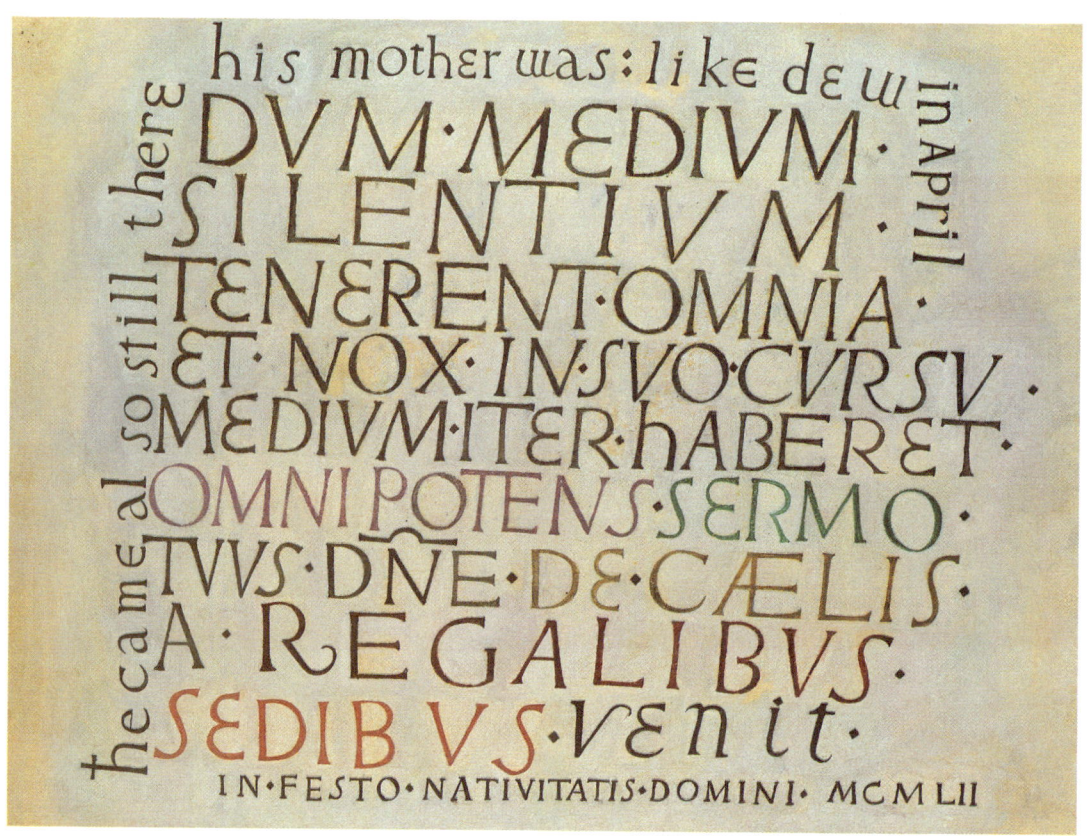

151 Dvm Medivm Silentivm 1952

Christ's Passion, the spear and the sponge, stand aslant within the chalice. According to Jessie Weston, the lance of the Grail story originally had nothing to do with the lance of Longinus which pierced Christ's side, but was an emblem of phallic potency, just as the cup originally signified the uterine resources of the female. Since in his annotations, Jones disagreed with this separation of meanings, we can be reasonably sure that he had both the sexual archetypes and the Christian symbols in mind when he engraved 'He Frees the Waters', as he certainly did when he drew 'Aphrodite in Aulis'.

In watercolours such as 'The Queen's Dish', 'Briar Cup' and 'Thorn Cup' (Cat. nos. 88, 93, 94), he circumvented the critical ban on any kind of literary symbolism by alluding to Grail motifs through ostensibly 'normal' still-life arranged upon a table. In most of these watercolours there is a degree of disorder, which may disturb eyes accustomed to the resolved beauty of the still-lifes of Nicholson or Nash. Indeed, Jones's are not still-lifes in any traditional sense: confronted by Cézanne's apples, we do not feel drawn to sit down and eat, yet in front of 'Linen Cloth' (Cat. no. 95), we notice the cloth has just been put on, the air still buoys it up, a meal is about to begin. Human presence and the vital disorder of life is everywhere implied. Out of the flux of light, forms emerge, firm and clear. In the 'Queen's Dish' the plate with apple and knife and fork may be 'the holy dysshe wherein I ete the lamb on Sherthursdaye';[36] the apple may recall the sin of Adam – the Happy Fault that necessitated the sacrifice of the second Adam, the *Agnus Dei*; the knife may signify the instrument with which the Victim was slain – for Jessie Weston maintains that the knife which is used in the oriental rite to divide the Eucharistic loaf corresponds to the instrument of wounding.

PIGOTTS AND
ROCK HALL

In 1928 Eric Gill moved from Capel-y-ffin to Pigotts, a farm-house surrounded by woods north of High Wycombe. Many of David Jones's watercolours of the next four years were painted here – not only views of the quadrangle of brick and timbered buildings (Cat. nos. 61, 69, 70, 84) but also flower pieces (Cat. no. 71), cows in 'The Long Meadow' (Cat. no. 90) which flanked the house, as well as portraits of Petra, Eric Gill, René Hague, Isabella Drummond and Prudence Pelham (Cat. nos. 83, 96, 65, 91, 82, 67). Apart from seaside Portslade and Caldy, and his parents' house in Brockley, the only other place in which he painted regularly in these years was Rock Hall in Northumberland, the home of Helen Sutherland. Jim Ede introduced David Jones to Helen Sutherland in 1928. In the following year he made the first of many long visits to the home of that remarkable patron. From the windows of the house he painted some of his most magical watercolours; on its walls he contemplated the finest collection of Ben Nicholson's early work.

While Jones's thoughts moved increasingly in a world of sacramental signs, myth and folk-tale, his eye's delight in particular beauties – the body in which he must clothe his vision – was undiminished. Of painting at Rock and Pigotts he wrote: 'I always work from the window of a house if it is at all possible. I like looking out on the world from a reasonably sheltered position. I can't paint in the wind, and I like the indoors-outdoors, contained yet limitless feeling of windows and doors. A man should be in a house; a beast should be in a field, and all that. The rambling, familiar, south, walled, small, flower-beddedness of Pigotts and the space, park, north, serene, clear, silverness of Rock in Northumberland both did something.'[37]

The lyricism of the watercolours was won against all odds. His quest for the grail was indeed perilous, beset with doubts. His drawings, his writings, and later his inscriptions, were fragments shored against his ruin. The difficulties derived from many quarters. A naturally nervous and sensitive temperament had been frayed and shocked by the appalling experience of the trenches. The reductionist utilitarianism of the modern world – the world of technics – seemed irreconcilably at odds with the sacramental vision of his faith. Painting too was dragged in the dust – 'isn't it awful', he lamented to Ede in 1929, 'these yards of "able" paintings of various kinds that seem only seen with the eye of the flesh.'[38] Amidst these difficulties, unable to reach a decision, the solace of the closest personal relationship was denied him. Philip Hagreen recalls the blow of Petra's decision to marry Denis Tegetmeier: 'David's boat was sailing with a fair wind towards a clear horizon. Then in January 1927 the mast snapped. Thereafter he could only row. He rowed bravely but, pulling at the oars, he could not see ahead. Denied the vision of hope he could only see what lay behind – the smouldering ruins of man's history and a litter of broken things.'[39]

Though Jones looked back over man's history, he was always struggling to give his works what he called 'nowness'. This modernity – never resting content with outworn modes – was to be most evident in his writing. It was a source of anguish in his visual art also. He never liked to repeat himself; he pushed forward however similar the subjects, so that if we compare flower-pieces separated by a year or less, we grow aware of subtle shifts of mood and handling. The struggle and anger is voiced in a letter of 1931 – 'been trying to paint but with no result save intolerable annoyance and rage . . . . Now going to try and paint usual flower business in sitting-room at H.Q. (the 'Big House' at Pigotts). I want a new vision – so tired.'⁴⁰

At first glance, the blues and pinks, the delicate flowers and fluttering curtains of 'Curtained Outlook' (Cat. no. 97) seem merely pretty. As our eye wanders over this strangely animated scene, it dawns that this is the vision of a man who experienced war, who had seen the solid earth dissolve – thrown skywards by an exploding shell. This world is recomposed, a vision of love triumphing in a desperate struggle against disintegration. In the uneven strokes, the spider cracks on the plaster wall, a sinister strain pulls against the sunlight. We are reminded of the disquieting, surreal, far from still, still-lifes of In Parenthesis:

> Slime-glisten on the churnings up, fractured earth pilings, heaped on, heaped up waste; overturned far throwings; tottering perpendiculars lean and sway; more leper-trees pitted, rownsepykèd out of nature, cut off in their sap-rising.
>
> Saturate, littered, rusted coilings, metallic rustlings, thin ribbon-metal chafing – rasp low for some tension freed; by rat, or wind, disturbed. Smooth-rippled discs gleamed, where gaping craters, their brimming waters, made mirror for the sky procession – bear up before the moon incongruous souvenirs. Margarine tins sailed derelict, where little eddies quivered, wind caught, their sharp-jagged twisted lids wrenched back.
>
> From chance hardnesses scintilla'd strikings, queer reboundings at spiteful tangent sing between your head and his.⁴¹

ILLUSTRATIONS TO 'IN PARENTHESIS'

The first draft of In Parenthesis was completed on 18 August 1932. Almost at the same time several months of intense painting (some sixty watercolours were completed that summer) were brought to an end by the onset of a nervous illness. This illness, the exact nature of which remains a mystery, was to afflict him with varying degrees of severity for the rest of his life. He never again painted so many watercolours in such a short space of time. More and more of his energies were spent in writing, and from the late 1940s onwards in the making of coloured inscriptions. Though he continued, at intervals, to draw from observed motifs, memory played an increasingly important role in his visual art and his physical circumstances mattered less. There is no change in direction in his work, but there is more than a technical development after the break of 1933. It is a progression from a lyrical to an epical form such as Joyce describes in Portrait of the Artist as a Young Man:

The lyrical form is in fact the simplest verbal vesture of an instant of emotion, a rhythmical cry such as ages ago cheered on the man who pulled at the oar or dragged stones up a slope... The simplest epical form is seen emerging out of lyrical literature when the artist prolongs and broods upon himself as the centre of an epical event and this form progresses till the centre of emotional gravity is equidistant from the artist himself and from others. The narrative is no longer purely personal. The personality of the artist passes into the narration itself, flowing round and round the persons and the action like a vital sea.[42]

It was in the writing of In Parenthesis that David Jones had brooded upon himself as the centre of an epical event. How could he find a visual form for the epical consciousness growing within him? The delicate, lyrical medium of watercolour seemed unsuited to bear so great a weight of meaning. Though no connection is proven it is at least suggestive that at the moment when he turned from the writing of In Parenthesis to its illustration, illness struck. 'I had intended to engrave some illustrations, but have been prevented', he laconically records in the preface.[43]

After an interval when nervous illness virtually prevented him from putting pen to paper, in 1936–7 he made several drawings for In Parenthesis, of which two were published as frontispiece and tailpiece (Cat. nos. 99, 100). They are the first of a series of densely packed, figurative drawings in which David Jones attempted to give bodily form to his sense of the continual presence of Divine Grace through all history. Since each drawing, under a variety of bodily 'accidents', shows forth the same eternal mystery, the meaning of each is illuminated by turning back and forth from one to another. In doing so we experience identity persisting through difference, which is very like the cumulative effect of reading The Anathemata. What bewilders at first as a tangled thicket of symbols may turn out to be a tended garden where no tree or flower has been planted without good reason.

Put at its simplest, and over-simplifying the complexity of theme, the major figurative images of 1937 to circa 1950 celebrate the Incarnation of Christ and His redemption of the world through his sacrifice on Calvary and his institution of the Eucharist, whereby that sacrifice is perpetually renewed. Just as in the Mass the historic present is one with the historic past, so also in David Jones's drawings. None of them 'illustrate' a single moment in time (one reason why traditional realism was out of place). The tailpiece to In Parenthesis alludes to the Scapegoat that was sent into the wilderness to bear away the sins of the world, but like the ram caught in the thicket and substituted for the sacrifice of Isaac, this ram is tangled in the barbed wire of No Man's Land. On the frontispiece the *Agnus Dei* is not yet wounded, the young soldier bears no marks of the stigmata. In some notes to an inscription Jones referred to a passage in *Piers Plowman* 'where Langland says that just as a man puts on his mail haubergeon, so our Lord put on human nature to "iouste in Iherusalem . . . (with) fals dome and deth".'[44] So it may be that the naked soldier's donning of his army jacket is a figure for Christ's assumption of the frailty of our mortal nature. The rest of the drawing reminds us of the battle he must do with falsedom and death: the fatigue parties recall the carrying of the Cross and the lopped and splintered trees, Calvary itself.

In *Parenthesis* was dedicated to, amongst others, 'the enemy front-fighters who shared our pains against whom we found ourselves by misadventure'. The Second World War stimulated David Jones to reaffirm the bonds that united the nations of Europe. The drawing, 'Epiphany 1941: Britannia and Germania embracing', (Cat. no. 113) is inscribed 'O sisters two what may we do', a line taken from the Coventry Carol, evidently in allusion to the devastation of that city by German bombs on the night of 14 November 1940. Coventry Cathedral, its spire struck down, appears on the left-hand side of the drawing. The Epiphany, the moment when the Messiah was revealed to the Gentiles, has always been regarded as symbolic of the unity of all nations, hence the appropriateness of the title.

The topical allusion of 'Epiphany 1941' is subsumed in a greater theme. As with the frontispiece and tailpiece to In *Parenthesis*, we are in the presence of sacred victims, wounded with the stigmata. Antlers crown the helmet of Germania, just as they were carried on the heads of mummers as they enacted the sacrifice of the tree-god, according to early German folk-tales. (Jones was well versed in tree-cults from his reading of Sir James Frazer's *Golden Bough*).

He had always been alert to architecture. He delighted to draw the mouldings and architectural ornaments of his parents' house, and recognized even in debased forms the survival so late in time of the orders. The language of architecture is easily taken for granted; Jones seized its sign-bearing power. At the opening of *The Anathemata*, the architectural metaphor underlines the loss of sacrality in the contemporary world:

Ossific, trussed with ferric rods, the failing numina of column
and entablature, the genii of spire and triforium, like great rivals met
when all is done, nod recognition across the cramped repeats of their
dead selves.[45]

The antithesis in 'Epiphany 1941' of the Gothic cathedral on the left and the Ionic capital on the right, more than an image of physical destruction, points to the ailing of Europe's classical and Christian culture. Later in the same year, Jones was immersed in Spengler's *Decline of the West*.

In the major drawing of the Second World War, 'Aphrodite in Aulis' (Cat.no.110) the contrasts of architectural orders, Classical, Egyptian, and Middle Eastern, which would never have been used in a single building, indicate that the goddess belongs to all times and all places. A preliminary study (Cat.no.111) suggests that Aphrodite is properly identified with the sacred enclosure, the *temenos*, of which she is the central column of breathing marble. Jones made play of such surrealist metamorphoses of flesh into marble, marble into flesh, in his writings – notably in *The Dream of Private Clitus*, a prose poem conceived at the same time as 'Aphrodite'. Classical precedent can be found, of course, in the caryatids of the Erechtheum and elsewhere.

APHRODITE: GODDESS AND COURTESAN

'Aphrodite in Aulis' may appear baffling in its complexity: once we recognize the inherent pictorial clue that its format is that of a Crucifixion we are on the road to understanding. The Tommy on the left bears, unmistakably, the lance of Longinus. Just as Christ on the Cross is both object of worship and victim of sacrifice, so also is Aphrodite. She stands, chained to the altar, part living flesh, with radiant stigmata, part statue, cracked like marble. The necessary theological connection between the institution of the Eucharist and the Passion of Christ, upon which Jones laid such emphasis, is expressed in bodily image by the juxtaposition of the relief of the *Agnus Dei* that bleeds into a chalice, immediately below the figure of the goddess. The implication that a Mass is in progress is made plain by the vested figure of the priest who censes the altar.

The universal significance of the drawing is sharpened, as is usual in Jones's work, by contemporary allusion. The British soldier on the left and the German on the right, identified by his helmet, the stick bombs tucked in his belt and the *fasces* – the Roman insignia of the fascist – upon his arm, are united in their love of the tutelary goddess. The soldier is Jones's eternal Everyman, as Saunders Lewis has noted:

> I suspect that David Jones would admit to two impressions that grew into part of his make-up. First that the soldier is the normal Western layman, the chap who has always been there when the Graeco-Latin civilization of the West has had its quarrels or has had to be defended. Anonymous, unknown, peasant or small town labourer, he sailed with

Odysseus, he fought at Philippi, he was at the Milvian Bridge, he was at Agincourt, he was a Desert Rat. He carries the tradition of three thousand years. He is timeless, old soldiers never die . . . And secondly, private soldier and Mother Earth belong to each other with an intimacy that not even the shepherd can know. He befouls her, he digs her, he sleeps on her, he lies on her in action and inaction, wounded and unwounded, alive, dying and dead. She is Matrona, Modron, Tellus, the Mother, and there's an invocation to her in the chapter of In Parenthesis where the battalion goes over the top:

>   mother earth
> she's kind:
> Pray her hide you in her deeps
> she's only refuge against
> this ferocious pursuer
> terribly questing.
> Maiden of the digged places
>   let our cry come unto thee.
> Mam, moder, mother of me
> Mother of Christ under the tree . . .[46]

So the Tommy and the Jerry are united in a love that is at once sacred and profane. Aphrodite is Mother and Bride; like Flora she is both goddess and courtesan. The soldiers may enjoy her favours: the Jerry is gartered as a lover, the lance of the Tommy carries the potency of the sexual archetype. The cleft stone, the *Agelastos Petra*, on the hillside at the left, signifies the female generative organ. If this seems to carry us far from theology, as with 'The Bride' and the 'Wounded Knight', it is still close to the spirit of the Song of Songs.

The final pages of In Parenthesis illumine these paradoxes. There David Jones drew an ironic parallel between violent death and the sexual act:

> But sweet sister death has gone debauched today and stalks on this high ground with strumpet confidence, makes no coy veiling of her appetite but leers from you to me with all her parts discovered.
>   By one and one the line gaps, where her fancy will – howsoever they may howl for their virginity
> she holds them – who impinge less on space . . .[47]

To enjoy the goddess's embraces is to be received into the bosom of mother earth and to share in the sacrifice of the sacred victim. At the close of In Parenthesis, when battle is done, the Queen of the Woods 'has cut bright boughs of various flowering' which she awards to the soldiers who strew the field. Doubtless these bright boughs are the Golden Bough of Vergilian fame, that will see them safely across the waters of death. In 'Aphrodite in Aulis' the German's rifle is bursting into leaf – his rod, like Aaron's, is budding – and in that bough, sacred wood of the Redeemer's Cross, lies his hope of salvation. Thus the drawing commemorates the soldiers of Britain and Germany who were at that moment dying in battle.

Whatever the ultimate universality of such symbolism it would be foolish to pretend its astonishing paradoxes were not distilled in the alembic of highly personal experience. The bodily form of Aphrodite herself is none other than the Venus de Milo which towered over the adolescent Jones's desk in the classroom at Camberwell School of Art. That he went to art school at fourteen rather than eighteen, as would be usual now, meant that at puberty his first exposure to the female nude was in the form of casts of goddesses of antiquity. When he progressed to the life class his imagination was trained to perceive in the living flesh of the model the lineaments of Aphrodite or Artemis. The average art student quickly forgot such things. For David Jones the abrupt transition from life-class to the all male world of the trenches seems to have reinforced this idealizing. The eminence afforded to the Virgin Mary by the Catholic tradition, which he embraced so soon after the First War, fitted with his own instincts. She became his essential mediatrix and protectress: all his drawings of archetypal women, Guinevere, Aphrodite and Flora, were to be variants of her litany.

His close friend René Hague has written of the dissolution of the engagement to Petra Gill: 'It was so obvious that marriage was out of the question, and that not only for financial reasons but also because David had known even from his teens that his vocation would not allow him to marry.'[48] It is tempting to conjecture that one reason for his enduring obsession with the Arthurian stories was due to an identification, largely unconscious I imagine, with the Grail questors. Their trials mirrored his own perplexities as a man highly susceptible to female beauty yet conscious of a vocational calling to celibacy. 'Aphrodite in Aulis' is drawn with a nervous, excited line. Its meaning transcends personal history, yet its vital confusion of the spiritual and the sexual reflects the inner tension of the artist. The emotional conviction of the draghtsmanship lifts such work far above the category of illustration.

The same may be said of two large drawings on Arthurian themes. David Jones spent most of the years 1935–40 at the Fort Hotel in Sidmouth, Devon, immersed in pessimism about the modern world and, to begin

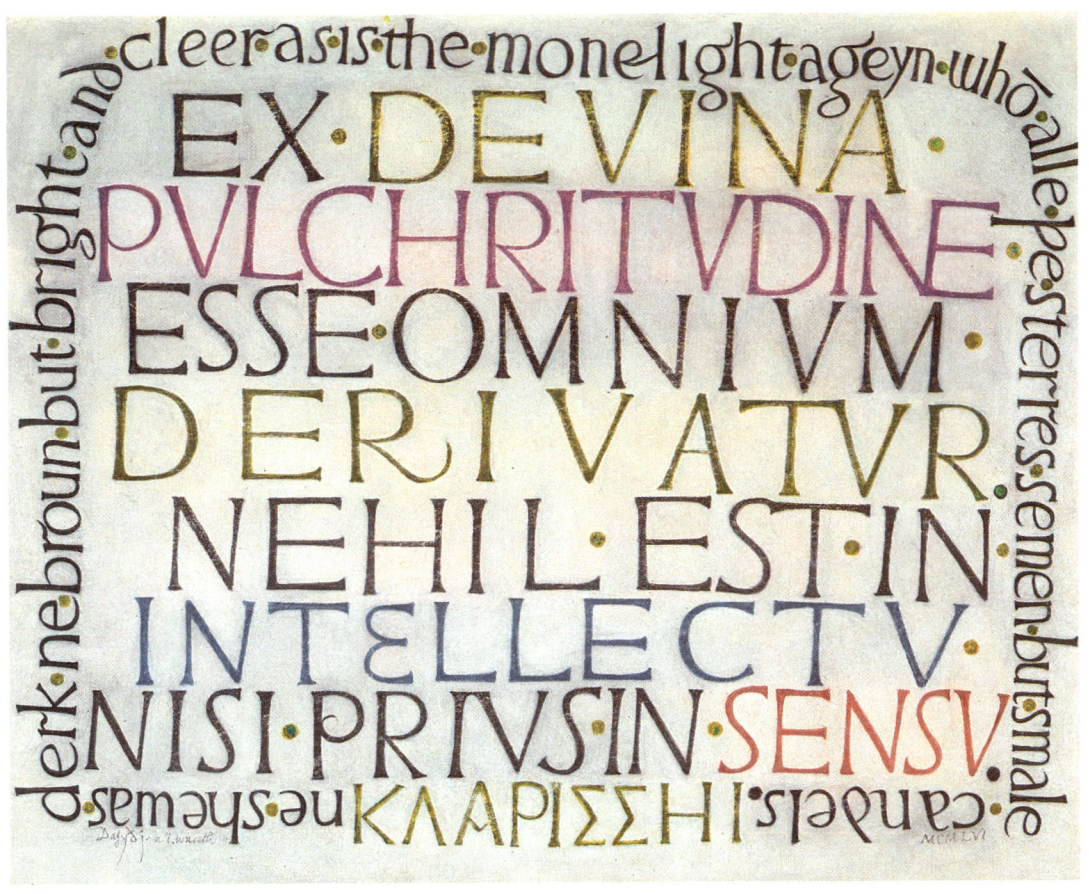

155   Ex Devina Pvlchritvdine 1956

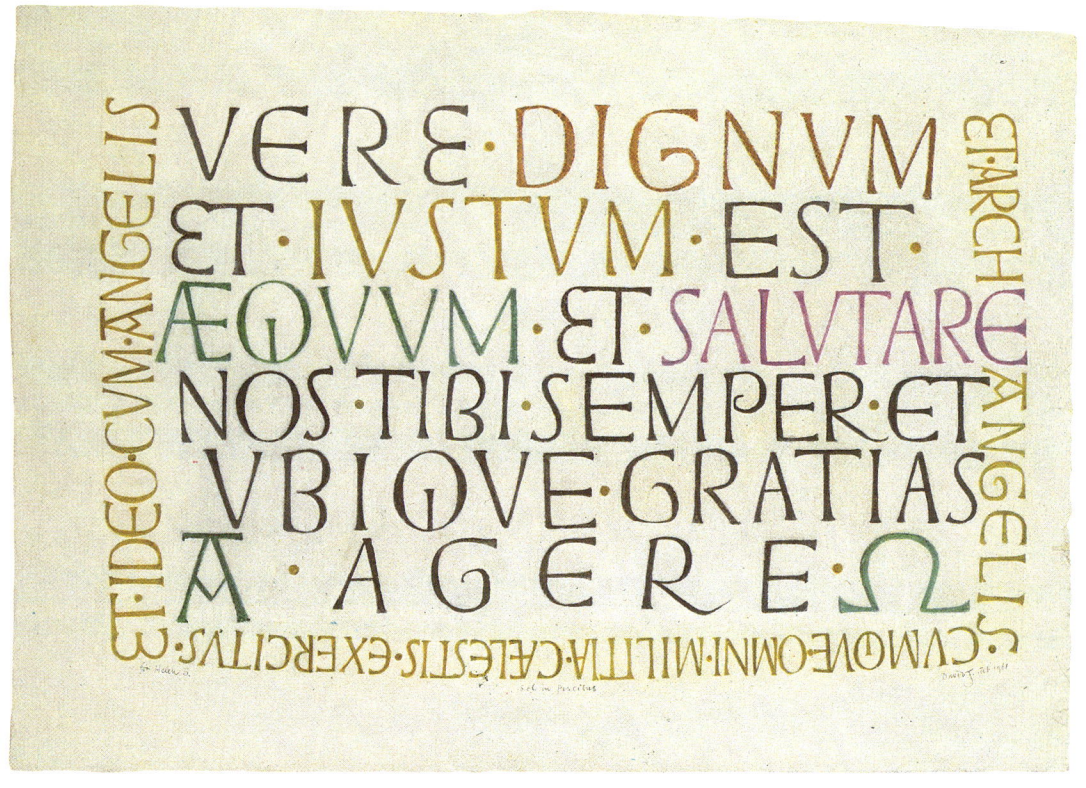

166 Vere Dignvm 1961

with, unable to draw. Douglas Cleverdon visited him at this seaside retreat and encouraged him – as a means of breaking the spell – to return to the Arthurian stories, this time not in engravings but in drawings and watercolours. The two subjects he eventually worked into finished pictures had personal and universal significance for him. Both tell the story of Launcelot, that most paradoxical of Grail heroes, flawed by his adultery yet marked as a type-figure for Christ. In 'Guenever' and the 'Four Queens find Launcelot Sleeping' we meet, as in 'Aphrodite in Aulis', the archetypal contrast of male and female principles, the soldier and the queen, enchantress or goddess of love. Launcelot, the Christian knight, is also the eternal soldier as a note to the 'Four Queens', approved by the artist, makes clear:

> The apple trees are associated with wire netting in the artist's mind, irrespective of the fact that there was no wire netting in the Middle Ages, while the recumbent figure of Launcelot reminds him of the bodies of soldiers on the battle-fields of the 1914–18 war: Launcelot wears a German helmet but his feet rest on a dog, an association with mediaeval tomb sculpture.[49]

We may understand 'Guenever' by approaching it through the imagery of The 'Bride' (Cat. no.16), The love of Launcelot and Guenever is analogous to that of Christ for his bride, the Church. The bed of Guenever is, figuratively, an altar; a spray of flowers lies upon it, as on the altar of Aphrodite; candles and crucifix surmount it. The reservation of the sacrament in the tabernacle on the altar in the background alludes to the perpetual renewal of Christ's union with His Church in the Eucharist. Since Launcelot is wounded with the stigmata as he breaks through the bars of the window, here, as in 'Aphrodite', the imagery of the Passion is linked to that of the Mass. The same theological purpose underlies the more direct imagery of his drawing of the Mass, entitled *A Latere Dextro* (Cat. no.129) in allusion to the water and blood that flowed 'from the right side' of Christ when he was pierced by the spear of Longinus.

THE LATER
GRAPHIC STYLE

Whereas in the late 1920s Jones attempted to keep in step with the most significant developments in contemporary art, after his breakdown in the autumn of 1932 this is harder to discern. The gulf between his own views of the nature of art and that of progressive critics, such as Herbert Read, widened. The Seven and Five Society under Nicholson's generalship turned more dogmatically in favour of abstraction. Jones's pictures were last shown at the Society's exhibition in 1933. Elements of Surrealism were, I have suggested, in tune with Jones's imagination, but Surrealism's enthronement of the subconscious and disregard for culturally based codes of meaning were inimicable to those very traditions that he believed it was the vocation of poets and artists to keep alive.

Jones's separation from the vital currents in contemporary visual art led to a slackening in the tempo of his own stylistic change. The new complexity in the figurative drawings of the forties reflects the ever-increasing range of under-tones and over-tones of which his remarkable imagination was aware. There are dangers in such imaginative cornucopia: coherence of design and clarity of meaning can so easily be lost when detail is piled on detail. 'Guenever' sails close to the wind in this respect. Whereas the early watercolours were often completed in three days, now they were drawn, rubbed and painted over months, sometimes years. Invention as well as execution extended through this time as Jones's perception of his subject deepened. We are familar with this process in terms of the oil painter's formal concerns (Matisse described it memorably), but less well prepared to follow the visual clues of an artist's ever-changing apprehension of meaning. Though preparatory studies preceded 'Aphrodite in Aulis', the ramifications of the subject were developed on the drawing itself. This involved a constant give and take between nuances of meaning and demands of design: as the drawing progressed certain details were strengthened with pencil or ink, or freckled with drily brushed watercolour or chalk or crayon, while other details were rubbed over, softened as though blurred by atmosphere. The result is an image that transmits sensations of light, air and wind, yet its constantly shifting focus offers an equivalent to the mind's changing perception of its multiplicity of signs.

This remained the style of Jones's figurative drawings as can be seen in 'Tristan ac Essyllt' (Cat. no.141) of 1962. It is worth noting that when he returned to drawing more spontaneously from the motif, as in 'View from Gatwick House, Essex', (Cat. no.117), he had lost none of his old mastery in conjuring light and space from contrasts of warm and cool colours. The colour, however, is never again as bold as it had been in 1930, in 'Pigotts Farm' (Cat. no.70) for instance. In the drawings of Cumberland of 1946 (Cat. no.116) there is a new transparency and a new sharpness in the delineation of stone walls, fences and branches. Any material density of colour would have spoilt this vision of the unity of all created things on these windy, rainswept moors.

The intense activity of the war years and the exhilaration of Cumberland were followed by the sudden return of his nervous illness. In 1947 he went

VEXILLA REGIS

for treatment at Bowden House, a private nursing home in Harrow. Whereas his doctors in the thirties had advised inactivity as the best cure, at Bowden he was urged to draw. Looking round for a motif, his eyes naturally came to rest upon the tall trees in the grounds of the house. Ever since he had been wounded in the attack on Mametz Wood in 1916, trees had been a living sign for him:

> Across the very quiet of no-man's-land came still some twittering. He found the wood, visually so near, yet for the feet forbidden by a great fixed gulf, a sight somehow to powerfully hold his mind. To the woods of all the world is this potency – to move the bowels of us.
>
> To groves always men come both to their joys and their undoing. Come lightfoot in heart's ease and school-free; walk on a leafy holiday with kindred and kind; come perplexedly with first loves – to tread the tangle frustrated, striking – bruising the green.

At first David Jones drew the trees with such delicacy we feel the sap rising in their limbs (e.g. Cat. no.119). Touches of chalk and wash hold a radiance suspended in their leaves. In October, the series culminated in the great 'Vexilla Regis', the meaning of which Jones explained in a long letter which is cited in the catalogue (no.122). If the picture's principal theme is the identification of the tree with the Cross of Christ, the sub-plot, which is inseparable from it, refers to the continuities bridging the Roman and Christian eras.

That the Roman *imperium* had acted as the womb of Christianity was a fact of tremendous significance for David Jones. In The Anathemata and in many of the pieces collected in The Sleeping Lord and Other Fragments he explored the paradoxical relationship between the temporal and spiritual empires. In 'The Mother of the West' (Cat. no.114) the Roman wolf gives suck not to Romulus and Remus but to the *Agnus Dei* – as explicit a bodily image as you could find of Christianity as heir to Rome. In Britain, the transition was identified in his imagination with those Romanized Britons, leaders of war-bands who had settled a particular tract of land. One such Arthurian figure whose name has been recorded is Cunedda Wledig, the Lord of Venedotia. The scarred Lord of his drawing of this name (Cat. no.123), of the year after 'Vexilla Regis', is a historical type, local and particular, of the universal Lord, the Harrower of Hell, evoked in Jones's poem The Hunt – he is

>   the diademed leader
>   who directs the toil
>   whose face is furrowed

> with the weight of the enterprise
>   the lord of the conspicious scars whose visage is fouled with
> the hog-spittle whose cheeks are fretted with the grime of the
> hunt-toil:
>   if his forehead is radiant
> like the smooth hill in the lateral light
>   it is corrugated
> like the defences of the hill
>   because of his care for the land
> and for the men of the land.[51]

In the drawing the Lord is also identified with the land, his forehead corrugated like the defences of the hill. The anthropomorphic analogy perceived in the mountains at Capel in the drawings of the twenties assumes a mythic dimension.

After the dominance of abstraction in the thirties, British art in the forties turned back to the romanticism of the native tradition. At a time of destruction – see the paintings of Piper and Sutherland for the War Artists' Advisory Committee – a care for roots and beginnings, the 'foretime' of Jones's *Anathemata*, was general. In his last paintings Nash wedded the English landscape to the foundational myths of Frazer's *Golden Bough*. Henry Moore uncovered the kinship, contemporary and primeval, of man and the land. Whatever the difference between their images, Moore's and Jones's imagination tunnelled the same continuities. It also seems likely that Jones's increasing use of chalk and crayon in the late forties owed something to the example of Moore's graphic style.

In the 'Lord of Venedotia' and other late drawings Jones contrived with a mixture of media a rubbed and worn texture that tells as metaphor for the fret and passage of time 'down the traversed history paths'. A visual image of the accumulation of deposits – a Cubist collage by Picasso read as archaeology – is discovered in *In Parenthesis* on the door of a billet:

LUX PERPETUA

> You bunch together before a tarred door. Chalk scrawls on its planking – initials, numbers, monograms, signs, hasty, half-erased, of many regiments. Scratched outdates measuring the distance back to antique beginnings.
>   Dragoons – one troop.
>   4th Hussars – 'D' Squadron No. 3 Troop.
>   Numerals crossed slanting indecipherable allocations earlier still.
>   More clear, and very newly chalked, you read the title of your

entering, and feel confident, as one who reads his own name in a church pew. '2 platoons, B Company', in large ill-formed calligraphy, countermanding the shadowy ciphering of the previous occupants.[52]

When, in the 1940s, Jones turned to shaping words in the form of inscriptions, he set some of them (Cat. nos. 144, 146, 147) against backgrounds textured with wax and chalk. Their beauty and meaning does not lie principally in this, but the visual effect of the endurance of the word – measuring the distance back to antique beginnings – is comparable to that of the figurative images.

Around 1950 the archaeological strain dies away. The words of the inscriptions stand out boldly on a field of Chinese white. The texts are often taken from the liturgy, particularly from the Mass, therefore they belong implicitly to the same world as the great series of drawings of flowers in a glass chalice. Anyone who has followed this far will soon apprehend the eucharistic nature of these watercolours. They take up the imagery of the cups and briars of 1932, but inessentials have dropped away. There is a new formality of placing – a ritual care. The pentecostal wind cannot shake the chalice, which stands as central in meaning as in design. Through the glassy orb of the chalice we see water, the element which first harboured life and without which there can be no flower and no seed. In 'Flora in Calix Light' (Cat. no.130) the surface of the water is blown in tiny ripples, which even as they raise their crests seem to become waves on the seas of the world – or on the Waterfall of Honddu – so that this chalice, like Marvell's Drop of Dew,

> ... recollecting its own Light,
> Does, in its pure and circling thoughts, express
> The greater Heaven in an Heaven less.

The 'Calix Light' of Jones's title is also the light of the Christmas Preface, part of which he inscribed as an illustration to *The Anathemata* (Cat. no.143): 'Quia per incarnati Verbi mysterium, nova mentis nostrae oculis lux tuae claritatis infulsit: ut dum visibiliter Deum cognoscimus, per hunc in invisibilium amorem rapiamur' (For through the mystery of the Word made flesh the new light of thy brightness has shone upon the eyes of our mind, so that as we see God in visible form, we are through him caught up into love of things invisible).

Though he was to paint for another ten years, the chalice drawings represent a peak that David Jones never surpassed. In them the universal shines forth from the particular; through visible forms we are caught up into love of things invisible. Some years earlier he had written: 'Cézanne . . . said we must "do Poussin again after nature". Perhaps we might almost say that we must do Cézanne's apples again, after the nature of Julian of Norwich's little nut, which "endureth and ever shall for God loveth it".'[53] As far as it was humanly possible David Jones had fulfilled that task.

[1] Eric Gill, *Last Essays*, London 1942, p.150
[2] Ibid., pp.151–2
[3] *Dying Gaul*, p.23
[4] p.120
[5] From notes made at Jim Ede's request for the Tate Gallery in 1935. The text was published in *David Jones: a memorial exhibition*, Kettle's Yard Gallery, University of Cambridge, 1975, (unpaginated)
[6] Letter quoted in R. Hague, *David Jones*, Cardiff 1975, p.56
[7] *Epoch and Artist*, p.297
[8] pp. VI–VII
[9] p.37
[10] p.12
[11] *The Anathemata*, p.79
[12] *Epoch and Artist*, p.30
[13] D. Attwater, *A Cell of Good Living*, London 1969, p.90
[14] In conversation with the author
[15] *Sleeping Lord*, p.74
[16] p.75
[17] *Dying Gaul*, p.140
[18] *Sleeping Lord*, p.64
[19] Letter to David Baxandall, 15 May 1949, in files of Manchester City Art Gallery
[20] *Agenda*, David Jones Special Issue, Autumn/Winter 1973/4, p.18
[21] Letter to Philip Hagreen, 26 March 1925, *Dai Greatcoat*, p.34
[22] *A Painter's Pilgrimage*, p.214
[23] *Drawing*, p.51
[24] *Agenda*, Twenty-first Anniversary: Ezra Pound Special Issue, 1979/80, p.274
[25] *Dying Gaul*, p.187
[26] Ibid., p.188
[27] Ibid., p.189
[28] *A Painter's Pilgrimage*, p.8
[29] *Dying Gaul*, p.190
[30] Ibid., p.198
[31] Same source as in note 5
[32] *The Anathemata*, p.41
[33] Copy in National Library of Wales, Aberystwyth
[34] p.XV
[35] *Dai Greatcoat*, p.46

36 Suggested by Malcolm Jones in *Lament for a Maker*, Cambridge BA, 1975, an unpublished thesis on David Jones to which I am much indebted
37 Same source as in note 5
38 *Dai Greatcoat*, p.46
39 Ibid., pp.41–2
40 Ibid., pp.49–50
41 pp.39–40
42 Penguin edition, p.214
43 p.XIII
44 Notes on the back of a photograph at Kettle's Yard, Cambridge, of CLOELIA CORNELIA
45 p.49
46 Aneiran Talfan Davies, *David Jones: Letters to a Friend*, Swansea 1980, pp.115–16; the quotation is from *In Parenthesis*, pp.176–7
47 p.162
48 *Dying Gaul*, p.42
49 *Tate Gallery Catalogue: Modern British paintings, drawings and sculpture*, I, London 1964, p.345
50 *In Parenthesis*, p.66
51 *Sleeping Lord*, p.67
52 p.22
53 *Dying Gaul*, p.142

CATALOGUE NOTE

The dimensions are given in inches followed by centimetres in brackets; height precedes width. Catalogue numbers marked with an asterisk indicate the work is reproduced in colour (see p.11).

In the section on inscriptions, the N.G. numbers given refer to Nicolete Gray's catalogue *The Painted Inscriptions of David Jones*, London 1981.

ENGRAVINGS & PRINTED ILLUSTRATIONS

1   ABSALOM 1922
      Wood-engraving, 3 x 3 (7.5 x 7.5)
      Douglas Cleverdon

The Death of Absalom illustrates the Commandment 'Honour thy father and thy mother'; published in *The Game*, St Dominic's Press, Ditchling.

2   MADONNA AND CHILD WITH
      OX AND ASS 1923
      Wood-engraving, $4\frac{1}{2}$ x 4 (11.5 x 10.2)
      Inscribed 'David Jones '23'
      Douglas Cleverdon

A progress proof.

3   THE GOOD SHEPHERD 1924
      Wood-engraving, $2\frac{3}{8}$ x $2\frac{3}{8}$ (6 x 6)
      Inscribed 'David Jones '24'
      Douglas Cleverdon

Bookplate for Clare and Hilary Pepler.

4   THE TOWN CHILD'S ALPHABET 1924
      Verses by Eleanor Farjeon
      Designs by David Jones
      The Poetry Bookshop 1924
      Douglas Cleverdon

Cover and 26 illustrations designed by Jones for line blocks in one, two and three colours.

5   ST FRANCIS AND THE WOLF 1925
      Copper-engraving, 3 x $2\frac{7}{8}$ (7.5 x 7.3)
      Douglas Cleverdon

Bookplate of 1925, inscribed
E. LIBRIS. W.H.F. SHEWRING

6   PONIES ON HILL-SLOPE 1926
      Copper-engraving, $4\frac{7}{8}$ x $5\frac{7}{8}$ (12.3 x 15)
      Inscribed 'David Jones '26'
      Douglas Cleverdon

This strong design – with its echo of the horses of Marc – was developed from a watercolour of

2

ENGRAVINGS & PRINTED ILLUSTRATIONS

Capel-y-ffin, 'Welsh Ponies', now in the Beaverbrook Art Gallery, Frederickton, New Brunswick, Canada. For the historic associations of the ponies, see no.41.

7

7   THE WHALE 1927
    Wood-engraving, $4\frac{1}{8}$ x $4\frac{7}{8}$ (10.5 x 12.3)
    National Museum of Wales, Cardiff

The seventh of thirteen engravings to *The Book of Jonah*, The Golden Cockerel Press, 1927; limited to 175 copies. A new edition, printed from the original blocks, was published in 1979 by Clover Hill Editions, 27 Barnsbury Square, N.1.

8   FLEET STREET
    Coloured line-blocks, 17 x $7\frac{3}{8}$ (43.2 x 18.7)
    Douglas Cleverdon

Broadside, with Jones's decorations to a poem by Shane Leslie, published by The Poetry Bookshop. The feet with radiant stigmata became a favourite motif.

9   FRONTISPIECE TO 'CHRISTIANITY AND ART'
    BY ERIC GILL 1927
    Wood-engraving, $4\frac{1}{2}$ x $2\frac{3}{4}$ (11.5 x 7)
    Douglas Cleverdon

10

Unsigned proof on japon. Jones's engraving is evidently modelled on evangelist portraits from Early Christian and Romanesque manuscripts such as the *Lindisfarne Gospels*. The marginalia of animals and birds show the fluency achieved as a result of the intensive study preparatory to illustrating *The Chester Play of the Deluge* (no.10).

10 THE DOVE 1927
    Wood-engraving, $6\frac{1}{2}$ x $5\frac{1}{2}$ (16.5 x 14)
    Inscribed 'Illus to Deluge 9th David Jones'27'
    Douglas Cleverdon

> My sweete dove to me brought hase
> a branch of olyve from some place

The ninth of ten engravings to *The Chester Play of the Deluge*, The Golden Cockerel Press, 1927; limited to 275 copies. A new edition was published in 1977 by Clover Hill Editions, 27 Barnsbury Square, N.1. Nicolete Gray wrote of 'The Dove',
'One can see the wonderful transparency of the sea, with the sense it conveys of the newness of the world washed clean; a sense repeated in the newly revived olive branches springing from the old and

[73]

broken tree ... It is the lines of the graver breaking up the black surface of the wood which have found the sea, in its newness. It is the different movement of the lines on the greater blackness that separate the growing tree from the formless waters below, and which again define the stability of the mountain beneath them. In all this the symbolism is very simple and fundamental. It is one to which we are all immediately susceptible, which is implicit in all art. Growth, newness, stability, movement ...'
('David Jones', *Signature*, N.S. 8, [1949], p.50).

11 THE LION AND THE FARMER 1928
Copper-engraving, $2\frac{1}{2}$ x $3\frac{1}{4}$ (6.4 x 8.3)
Douglas Cleverdon

Jones engraved seven plates to illustrate *Seven Fables of Aesop*, translated from Greek into English by W.H. Shewring, Lanston Monotype Corporation, 1928. According to the colophon, 150 copies were printed; actually there were only 50.

12 NATIVITY WITH BEASTS AND SHEPHERDS 1928
DUM MEDIUM SILENTIUM TENERENT OMNIA
Dry-point, $6\frac{3}{4}$ x $5\frac{3}{8}$ (17.2 x 13.7)
Inscribed 'Sunday within the Octave of Xmas, 1928. David J. '28'
Douglas Cleverdon

In 1927 Jones first engraved in dry-point, a technique in which the burr, or shaving of metal forced up by the burin, is not removed. Since the burr attracts the ink, dry-points tend to print an uneven, scratchy line – a quality Jones exploits to advantage in this Christmas card. The composition resembles that of El Greco's *Agony in the Garden*, a painting which made a great impression on Jones when it entered the National Gallery in 1921. As in the Byzantine tradition, to which El Greco harked back, this Nativity is set within a cave; by identifying the Virgin with the rocks that enclose her, Jones likens her to *Tellus Mater*, the earth mother, who is both womb and grave. An allusion to El Greco's Gethsemane may not be unintended since, according to Jones's view of Catholic theology, Christ's Passion was comprehended in his Incarnation (c.f. Cat. no. 14) – the cave of the Nativity and the cave of the Sepulchre symbolically are one. The inscription *Dum medium* . . . is taken from the Mass of the Sunday after Christmas; the same words were chosen for a painted inscription for Christmas 1952 (see no.151).

13 THE RIME OF THE ANCIENT MARINER 1929
Eight copper-engravings, illustrating the poem by Samuel Taylor Coleridge,
each $6\frac{7}{8}$ x $5\frac{3}{8}$ (17.5 x 13.7)
Douglas Cleverdon

The Ancient Mariner with Jones's engravings, was published by Douglas Cleverdon at Bristol in 1929. The engravings exhibited here are from the extra set printed on handmade paper for the Clover Hill edition of 1964. According to Cleverdon this was the only set of which Jones totally approved. The small head-piece and tail-piece are omitted. On technique and style, see the artist's discussion in 'An Introduction to the Rime of the Ancient Mariner' (*Dying Gaul*, pp.186-225), which is quoted in the introduction to this catalogue, p.45

i The Wedding Guests

It is an ancient Mariner,
And he stoppeth one of three,
'By thy long grey beard and glittering eye,
Now wherefore stopp'st thou me?'

ii The Albatross

In mist or cloud, on mast or shroud
It perched for vespers nine;
Whiles all the night, through fog-smoke white,
Glimmer'd the white Moon-shine.

'God save thee, ancient Mariner!
From the fiends, that plague thee thus! –
Why look'st thou so?' – 'With my cross-bow
I shot the ALBATROSS!'

iii The Death-Fires

The very deep did rot: O Christ!
That ever this should be!
Yea, slimy things did crawl with legs
Upon the slimy sea.

About, about, in reel and rout
The death-fires danced at night;
The water, like a witch's oils,
Burnt green, and blue and white.

ENGRAVINGS & PRINTED ILLUSTRATIONS

13ii

iv Life-in-Death

This Ship it was a plankless thing,
A bare Anatomy!
A plankless Spectre – and it mov'd
Like a Being of the Sea!
The woman and a fleshless man
Therein sate merrily.

v The Curse

An orphan's curse would drag to Hell
A spirit from on high;
But oh! more horrible than that
Is the curse in a dead man's eye!
Seven days, seven nights, I saw that curse,
And yet I could not die.

vi The Mariners

The helmsman steered, the ship moved on;
Yet never a breeze up-blew;
The mariners all 'gan work the ropes,
Where they were wont to do;
They raised their limbs like lifeless tools –
We were a ghastly crew.

vii The Town

O dream of joy! is this indeed
The light-house top I see?
Is this the hill? is this the kirk?
Is this mine own countree?

viii Vespers

O sweeter than the marriage feast,
'Tis sweeter far to me,
To walk together to the kirk
With goodly company! —

14 NATIVITY WITH SHEPHERDS AND BEASTS
REJOICING 1930
ANIMETUR GENTILIS
Copper-engraving, 8 x 6¼ (20.3 x 16)
National Museum of Wales

14

A Christmas card, intended for 1929 but not finished until 1930. In 'A Christmas Message 1960' Jones wrote, 'The Incarnation and the Eucharist cannot be separated; the one thing being analogous to the other. If one binds us to the animalic the other binds us to artefacture and both bind us to

[75]

signa, for both are a showing forth of the invisible under visible signs.' (*Dying Gaul*, p.171). In this Nativity, a cow bends tenderly towards its calf: such creaturely analogy for the care of the Blessed Virgin for her Firstborn Son is typical of the engraver's sympathy for 'the common travail of all creation'. The cockerel and birds, who join in the music of the shepherds, are doubtless the 'Celestiall Fowlis' of Dunbar – see the painted inscription no. 167. The cauldron and ladle, and the sheaf of corn which is the Virgin's bolster, underline the identity of the Incarnation and the Eucharist. The girl – foretype of Mary Magdalen – who carries the sacrificial lamb, the *Agnus Dei*, alludes to the same theme.

15   WOUNDED KNIGHT 1930 (?)
      Dry-point, $7\frac{7}{8}$ x $6\frac{1}{4}$ (20 x 16)
      Inscribed '1930 (?) David Jones'
      Douglas Cleverdon

Artist's proof; later there was an edition of 50 signed prints. This dry-point was a trial run for an illustrated *Morte Darthur* (see introduction p.49).
Its meaning is illuminated by Jones's description of the Celtic goddess Arianrhod as –
'a virgin-mother, of a kind, she gave birth to Dylan, which means a wave of the ocean. In Wales the Milky Way is called after her, Caer Arianrhod, Arianrhod's Fort. In Layamon's Middle English poem, the Brut, she is called "Argante queen of Avallon" and it is to her that Arthur is taken, after the battle of Camlann, to be healed of his death wound. She is referred to by the bards as a particularly shining and radiant beauty. She is associated with a wave-washed island or spit of land. She may have been the presiding deity of the Celtic Otherworld'. (From notes on the back of a photograph of the inscription CLOELIA CORNELIA.)

16   THE BRIDE 1930
      Wood-engraving, $4\frac{1}{2}$ x $3\frac{1}{4}$ (11.4 x 8.2)
      Private collection

Frontispiece to *Hermia and Other Poems* by W. H. Shewring, St Dominic's Press, 1930. See introduction, p.50. The dual nature of the Bride as the Virgin Mother and as courtesan was in the poet's mind when he imagined the celebrated courtesans of antiquity, Phryne and Lais, entering a church to say a quick decade of the rosary: *The Anathemata*, p.180. The

15

16

ENGRAVINGS & PRINTED ILLUSTRATIONS

sacred imagery of the woodcut is brought together in a manuscript draft of *The Anathemata* (no.171):

> he her groom that was his mother
> > he who cries
>
> > as the stag *ad fontes*
> > his desiderate cry

17 HE FREES THE WATERS IN HELYON 1932
Unfinished wood-engraving, 6 x 9½ (15.2 x 24.1)
Douglas Cleverdon

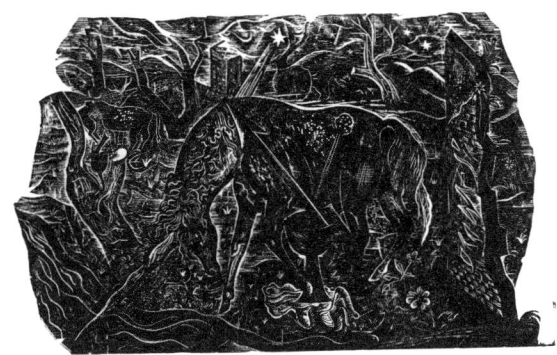

See introduction pp.50–5. The engraving was used as an illustration to *The Anathemata*, where the Unicorn, a type for Christ, is alluded to many times, (e.g. pp.136, 207 and 225). 'Freer of the Waters' is included amongst the Redeemer's titles in the inscription WHAT SAYS HIS MABINOGI (no.162). The mythological background is given in a note to the lines of *In Parenthesis*:

> I am the Single Horn thrusting
> > by night-stream margin
> > in Heyon. (p.84)

'In the fields of Helyon there is a river called Marah, the water of which Moses struck with his staff, and made the waters sweet, so that Israel might drink. And even in our time, it is said, venomous animals poison that water at the setting sun, so that good animals cannot drink of it, but in the morning, after sunrise, comes the Unicorn, and dips his horn into the stream, driving the Venom from it, so that the good animals can drink there during the day.'
(*Itinerarium Joannis de Hesse*)

BOXWOOD CARVINGS

In the mid 1920s, David Jones made a number of small end-grain boxwood carvings, 'things which alone would place him in the first rank of modern artists' (Eric Gill, *Last Essays*, p.151). This was a natural extension of wood-engraving, indeed it is probable that several of the carvings were made from discarded blocks. Jones liked working on this small scale, accommodating to the hand. The carvings were not intended for sale or for exhibition, and none appears to have been made after the 1920s.

[77]

18 TORSO c.1924–6
   Boxwood, 3½ high (8.9)
   Private collection

19 MATER CASTISSIMA 1924
   Boxwood, 4½ x 2⅞ (11.4 x 7.3)
   Lit: N. Gray, 'David Jones and the art of lettering', Motif, 7, (1961), pp.69–80
   Philip Hagreen

Philip Hagreen, who worked alongside Jones at Ditchling, writes,
'he followed Eric in working old blocks into reliefs. He made a *Mater Castissima*, a tiny thing of monumental majesty. But when he wanted to make a base he was flummoxed. To fasten two pieces of wood together was almost carpentry. I had to do that.'
(*Dai Greatcoat*, p.29)

The text on the back of the carving reads:
   O VIRGO VIRGINVM QUOMODO FIET ISTVD
   QVIA NEC PRIMAN SIMILEM VISA ES
   NEC HABERE SEQVENTEM.
   FILIAE JERVSALEM QVID ME ADMIRAMINI
   DIVINVM EST MYSTERIVM HOC QVOD
   CERNITIS

David Jones took this text from the Advent Vespers Magnificat antiphon which forms part of the Little Office of Our Lady. This used to be said at the workshops at Ditchling.

19

20 CRUCIFIXION c.1925
   Boxwood, 4½ x 3 (11.4 x 7.6)
   Lit: R. Hague, *David Jones*, Cardiff 1975, p.24;
   R.L. Charles, 'David Jones – Some Recently Acquired Works,' *Amgueddfa: Bulletin of the National Museum of Wales*, 22, Spring 1976, pp.4–5
   National Museum of Wales, Cardiff

R.L. Charles pointed out that the flanking figures represent the Old and New Testaments. 'The Old Testament holds the scroll of the Law, and the New Testament catches Christ's blood in a chalice.' It is likely that the block was originally worked for an engraving since the blood issues from the left rather than the right side – *A Latere Dextro* – of Christ's body. This would have been reversed, and so corrected, in a print.

21   MADONNA AND CHILD 1925–6
     Wood, 4 x 3 (10.1 x 7.6)
     Mrs D. Tegetmeier

22   PROFILE HEAD OF PETRA GILL 1925–6
     Wood, 3¾ x 3 (9.5 x 7.6)
     Mrs D. Tegetmeier

23   SANCTA HELENA O.P.N. c.1926
     Wood, 2¼ x 1 (5.7 x 2.5)
     Mrs D. Tegetmeier

St Helena, the mother of Constantine the Great, was the discoverer of the Wood of the True Cross. This pendant, carved on both sides, was given to Petra Helen Gill (c.f. no.115).

DRAWINGS & PAINTINGS

24

24   DANCING BEAR 1903
     Pencil, 20 x 10¾ (50.8 x 27.3)
     Inscribed 'David Jones, aged 7, 1903'
     Kulgin Duval and Colin H. Hamilton

In the penultimate year of his life, Jones spoke of his childhood drawings: 'Animals were what I usually drew, and the dancing bear, a drawing from the window in 1902 of one of those brown bears that used to be brought round the streets and roads by keepers seeking to earn a pittance, is still, I think, my favourite drawing.' (*Dying Gaul*, p.24). On the evidence of this drawing he averred – with some justification – that the essentials of his style were formed by the age of seven.

25   LANDSCAPE IN KENT
     Oil, 27¾ x 35¾ (70.5 x 90.8)
     Inscribed 'DJ 21'
     Private collection

This oil, unusually close in feeling to the earliest post-war landscapes of John and Paul Nash, shows the level of academic competence Jones had attained before his style was 'purged' at Ditchling.

26   JESUS MOCKED 1922–3
     Oil on tongue-and-groove boards,
     44⅛ x 41½ (112.1 x 105.4)
     Guild of St Joseph & St Dominic

DRAWINGS & PAINTINGS

A small-scale replica is signed 'DJ 23 AD', therefore the original must date from 1922 or early 1923. As Paul Fussell points out (*The Great War and Modern Memory*, Oxford 1975, pp.117–20), the Passion of Christ was frequently in the minds of the soldiers in the Great War. The wayside Calvaries of Flanders aroused, in Robert Graves's words, 'a sympathetic reverence for Jesus our fellow-sufferer'. Jones, however, in painting one of the mockers of Christ with the helmet of the Tommy intended to draw a parallel between the modern soldier and the Roman legionary rather than between the soldier and Christ. The soldiers dance around the Man of Sorrows, and one, the Longinus of the scene, drops on one knee as if his mocking had turned to reverent genuflection. The soldiers' predicament is typic of that of all mankind – responsible through sin for the Passion, yet given thereby hope of redemption. Such theologically meaningful ambivalence was developed more fully by Jones in *The Tribune's Visitation* and *The Fatigue* (both printed in *The Sleeping Lord*).

26

27 ELIZABETH, PETRA AND JOANNA GILL 1924
    Pencil and wash, $11\frac{1}{4}$ x $15\frac{5}{8}$ (28.6 x 39.7)
    Inscribed 'For Eric and Mary from David Michael. Easter 1924 A.D.'
    'David Michael J. Easter 1924 A.D.'
    Anthony d'Offay

The format of the three profiles is modelled on Gill's own drawing of his three daughters of 1914 (reproduced in Eric Gill, *Autobiography*, London 1940, opposite p.172). Given the repetition of the inscription, and the solemnity of the heads, it is just possible that Jones had in mind the three women who came to the sepulchre early on Easter morning.

27

28 THE GARDEN ENCLOSED 1924
    Oil on panel, 14 x $11\frac{3}{4}$ (35.6 x 29.8)
    Inscribed 'David Jones '24'
    Lit: *The Tate Gallery 1974–6: Illustrated Catalogue of Acquisitions*, London, 1978, pp.114–16
    Tate Gallery

The title alludes to the *Song of Solomon* iv:12, 'A garden inclosed is my sister, my spouse'. The enclosed garden is a common figure for the virginity

[80]

DRAWINGS & PAINTINGS

of Mary. The artist portrays himself embracing Petra Gill in the garden of the Crank at Ditchling. The geese – sacred to Juno – sound the alarm; a doll thrown down may indicate the end of childhood.

29 TIR Y BLAENAU Dec./Jan. 1924–5
    Pencil, ink and watercolour,
    22½ x 15 (57.1 x 38.1)
    National Library of Wales, Aberystwyth

Jones translated the title as 'land of the border uplands' (Sleeping Lord, p.95). Drawn soon after his arrival at Capel-y-ffin, in December 1924, this shows the terrain later evoked in many passages of the Sleeping Lord. In In Parenthesis (p.77) he wrote: 'The water in the trench-drain ran as fast as stream in Nant Honddu in the early months, when you go to get milk from Pen-y-Maes.'

30 SANCTUS CHRISTUS DE CAPEL-Y-FFIN 1925
    Gouache, 7½ x 5⅛ (19 x 13)
    Inscribed 'DMJ 25'
    Edgar Holloway

An image of wooden simplicity, not so much a 'picture' of the Crucifixion, as a rough-hewn wayside shrine, set in the Black Mountains. By distancing his work from realism, Jones uncovers signs: the limbs of Christ are like the branches of the Cross, which have been hewn from the trees on the mountainside. The painted inscriptions originated from within the context of such images.

29

31 TENBY FROM CALDY ISLAND 1925
    Watercolour and bodycolour,
    13½ x 20½ (34.3 x 52)
    Inscribed 'David J '25'
    National Museum of Wales, Cardiff

A composition of bold shapes is moulded round an empty centre and enlivened by small dark accents – a stylistic feature which becomes increasingly important. Jones stayed on Caldy for the first time in March and April 1925. The plantation of new trees which he wrote about with such excitement to Philip Hagreen (see introduction p.36–7), may be the grove on the left of this watercolour.

30

[81]

DRAWINGS & PAINTINGS

32   A TOWN GARDEN 1926
     Pencil and watercolour, 22½ x 14½ (57.1 x 36.8)
     Inscribed 'David Jones'26'
     The Loftus Collection

Drawn from his parents' house in Howson Road, Brockley; see introduction, p.31.

33   THE SUBURBAN ORDER 1926
     Pencil and watercolour, 15 x 21 (38.1 x 53.3)
     Inscribed 'David Jones '26'
     Portsmouth City Museums and Art Gallery

Drawn at Brockley, probably in April or early May.

34   THE MAID AT NO.37 1926
     Pencil and watercolour, 15¾ x 11 (40 x 28)
     Inscribed 'David Jones '26 (May)'
     National Museum of Wales, Cardiff

R.L. Charles wrote of this and other Brockley watercolours of 1926–8:
'They are pictures of delight in the orderliness, the very homeliness, of small gardens and front rooms. The artist has by now found his direction. The contrast with the stern immature contrivance of the Ditchling drawings could hardly be greater. The line and the colour combine in a gentle flowing motion over the paper. As Arthur Howell wrote, here is "a charm, an imponderable delicacy and gentleness of vision, maturely handled, that was entirely personal". The unambitious subjects, for all their casualness and gentle humour, are presented with evident craftsmanship of composition. Notice, for example, the procession of diagonals zigzagging up the sheet, in counterpoint to the more obvious verticals and horizontals; the flow of the line of the branch continued along the girl's shoulder; the way that the shape of her head and cap is echoed in that of her wash-leather, and how the line of her bottom rhymes with that of the bending boughs. As for the beribboned cat, David Jones had throughout his life a particular fondness for animals, and drew them as friends, even the rats of the trenches.'
('David Jones – Some Recently Acquired Works', *Amgueddfa: Bulletin of the National Museum of Wales*, 22, [1976], p.5)

31

32

DRAWINGS & PAINTINGS

33

35

35 THE DOG ON THE SOFA 1926
Pencil and watercolour, 21 x 15 (53.3 x 38.1)
Inscribed 'David Jones 1926'
National Museum of Wales, Cardiff

A view of the Edwardian interior of his parents' dining-room at Brockley, seen through the lens of Picasso, Braque and Matisse.

36 GARDEN AT BROCKLEY 1926
Pencil and watercolour, 24½ x 18½ (62.2 x 47)
Inscribed 'David Jones '26'
T.F. Burns

As with many of his drawings, Jones never gave this one a title, referring to it in a letter as 'Garden at Brockley with big tree in summer and cat walking on wall' (*Dai Greatcoat*, p.127). Unlike the drawings made in the spring of 1926 (nos.32, 33), here the artist's eye is more selective, so that tree and cat become the subject of the picture rather than its incidental content. In this it foreshadows the great tree studies of 1947 (nos.120–2), though it can hardly yet be freighted with their burden of meaning.

*37 THE WATERFALL, AFON HONDDU FACH 1926
Pencil and watercolour, $21\frac{7}{8}$ x $14\frac{7}{8}$ (55.5 x 37.8)
Inscribed 'David Jones 1926 June'
Lit: *Word and Image*, no.30
Whitworth Art Gallery,
University of Manchester

c.f. *The Anathemata*, p.235:

                  Stands a lady
  on a mountain
           who she is
they could not know.
His waters were in her pail
her federal waters ark'd him.
He by whom the welling *fontes*
    are from his paradise-font mandated
to make virid Gwenfrewi's glen, Dyfrdwy
to crystal his ferned Hodni dell
      dewy for the Dyfrwr
by this preclear and innocent creature.

Notes to this passage: 'Drayton speaks of St David drinking of the "crystal Hodni". This is the same river as the Honddu after which Llanthony is named.

[83]

Llan Dewi Nant Honddu, the "enclosure of David in the dingle of the Honddu". This stream is crystal clear and its banks are ferny. David had a cell there . . . Y Dyfrwr is the Welsh word for Aquarius, and St David is called Dewi Ddyfrwr, David the Waterman.' (A draft of the opening of this passage is exhibited amongst the manuscripts of *The Anathemata* [see no. 171].)

Though the imagery of Christ as the living water may not yet, in 1926, have been associated with this waterfall, the watercolour does offer a foretype of the chalice drawings of c.1950, in which the crystal-clear water is also whitened with body colour. Compare also the words of the inscription MULIER CANTAT (see no. 165).

38   MR GILL'S HAY HARVEST 1926
     Pencil and watercolour, $22\frac{1}{2}$ x 15 (57.1 x 38.1)
     Inscribed 'David Jones '26'
     T. L. Taylor

This view looking up towards the monastery and chapel at Capel-y-ffin is a rarity in that it shows figures worked into the rhythm of the composition. A sketch, dated 26 August, indicates the planning that went into this seemingly casual picture. Whereas the buildings are still treated schematically, there is a new vigour in the drily brushed flecks of colour which model the nearest haystacks.

39   GOATS ON A MOUNTAINSIDE 1926
     Pencil and watercolour, 22 x $15\frac{1}{4}$ (55.9 x 38.7)
     Inscribed 'David Jones '26'
     Miss Jaqueline Hope Wallace, CBE

Eric Gill brought goats from Ditchling to Capel-y-ffin (*Autobiography*, London 1940, p.216) where they grazed not far from the monastery. Jones made a large number of drawings of animals in 1926, which formed the basis for the engravings to the *Chester Play of the Deluge*.

40   THE SPEED OF THE HIPPO 1926
     Pencil and watercolour, 4 x $9\frac{3}{4}$ (10.1 x 24.8)
     Inscribed 'DMJ '26'
     Mrs D. Tegetmeier

A dispute about the speed of the hippopotamus between David Jones and Denis Tegetmeier led to this illustration in the spirit of Belloc. Tegetmeier runs away, while Jones sticks to his sketching board.

41   HILL PASTURES, CAPEL-Y-FFIN 1926
     Pencil, watercolour and chalk,
     $14\frac{3}{4}$ x $21\frac{1}{2}$ (37.5 x 54.6)
     Inscribed 'David Jones '26'
     Lit: Blamires, pp.52–3; *Word and Image*, no.28;
     E. Gray, *Agenda*, Winter—Spring 1975, pp.127–8
     Helen Sutherland Collection

As in the copper-engraving, 'Ponies on a Hill-Slope' (no.6), the profiles of the ponies are rhymed with the contours of the hills, particularly the central Tump (Y Twmpa). Cross-hatching, an engraver's technique, is applied extensively. The curious interlocking of bare tree, cottage and hillside, on the right, suggests that Jones was already appreciative of Ben Nicholson's 'quasi-abstraction'. The ubiquitous Welsh ponies carried the poet's mind back to the end of Arthurian Britain, when the horses of Arthur's knights ran free after the disastrous battle of Camlann: 'Those straying riderless horses gone to grass in forest and on mountain, seem as their masters to have acquired a new yet aboriginal liberty. We seem to have seen their descendants, shrunken in bulk, as happens to all creatures that the highland zone assimilates, but holding themselves with breeding, black in colour, and primitive in contour, on a Brecon hill-slope . . .'
(*Epoch and Artist*, p.251)

42   Y TWMPA, NANT HONDDU 1926
     Pencil and watercolour, 22 x $15\frac{1}{8}$ (55.9 x 38.4)
     Inscribed 'David Jones '26 Capel'
     Anthony d'Offay Gallery

See no.41

40

42

DRAWINGS & PAINTINGS

44

43 THE SEA WALL 1927
Pencil, watercolour and gouache,
13 x 18¾ (33 x 47.6)
Inscribed 'David Jones Jan '27'
H.R. Allen

An unusually sombre painting of Caldy.

44 ROCKS AND SURF, CALDY 1927
Pencil and watercolour, 13⅜ x 19⅛ (34 x 48.5)
Inscribed 'David Jones '27'
Private collection

The broad sweep of this composition is firm yet full of movement, calling to mind the lines of *The Anathemata* (p.77),

> As though the sea itself were sea-borne
> and under weigh

45 WILD BOAR
Pencil and watercolour, 9⅝ x 13 (24.4 x 33)
Inscribed 'David Jones '27'
Private collection

This watercolour may have been developed from one of the studies for *The Chester Play of the Deluge*: two boars appear in the fifth engraving. *Culhwch and Olwen*, the early Welsh tale of the hunting of the boar, was reworked by Jones in his poem *The Hunt* (*The Sleeping Lord*, pp.65–9).

46 BRIGHTON 1927
Pencil and watercolour, 15 x 19¾ (38.1 x 50.2)
Inscribed 'David Jones '27 Brighton'
Private collection

In 1927, Jones stayed in a seaside villa at Portslade, which was rented for the summer by his parents. He first drew the view looking east, towards Brighton; in later years, he preferred to stay indoors and use the terrace as a frame (see nos. 60, 80). This freely drawn watercolour shows how his style was loosening in 1927. The sight of the white cliffs, just visible beyond the piers, was recalled in *The Narrows*:

> And on the heights above the spume-fret
> the albescent chalk
>   cliffs gleam-bright
> her sea-ward parapets.
>   It was, he said, as though the White Island
> lay at anchor
>   riding a mooring
> just off Europa's main.
> And had so lain
>   for countless millennia back
> and would so lie
>   hodiern, modern, sempitern.

(*Agenda*, David Jones Special Issue, 1973–4, p.14)

52

47 PATH BY THE COAST 1927
Pencil and watercolour, $21\frac{1}{2} \times 14\frac{3}{4}$ (54.6 x 37.5)
Inscribed 'David Jones '29'
Private collection

A letter from the Redfern Gallery of November 1936 states, 'I've at last got David Jones to sign your picture'. Since there is no other record that the artist visited Caldy – the subject of the watercolour – at any time between November 1927 and the autumn of 1931, it is probable that Jones's dating was mistaken. Stylistically, this watercolour belongs to the autumn of 1927.

48 DEER NIBBLING AT STRAW c.1927
Pencil and chalk, $16\frac{1}{2} \times 20\frac{1}{2}$ (41.9 x 52)
Mr and Mrs Christopher Hull

This drawing on glossy paper may possibly be in silver-point rather than pencil.

49 ELEPHANT 1928
Pencil and watercolour, $14 \times 17\frac{5}{8}$ (35.5 x 44.8)
Inscribed 'David Jones '28'
Private collection

One of a large number of drawings made at London Zoo (c.f. nos. 75, 76, 77).

50 DEER 1928
Pencil and chalk, $15\frac{3}{4} \times 20\frac{7}{8}$ (40 x 53)
Inscribed 'David Jones '28'
Private collection

51 LOURDES 1928
Bodycolour, $18\frac{7}{8} \times 23\frac{5}{8}$ (48 x 60)
Inscribed 'David Jones '28'
Kettle's Yard, Cambridge

In the early summer of 1928 Jones travelled with Gill to south-west France. This view of the great pilgrimage centre of Lourdes was painted while he was staying with Philip Hagreen at Chalet St Vincent, Monastère des Dominicaines. Working in a gouache medium, he combined elements from Cézanne (notably in the left foreground) with a directness and naïveté characteristic of children's art. That directness was particularly suited to this subject.

DRAWINGS & PAINTINGS

52 RIVER GAVE IN THE PYRENEES 1928
   Pencil and watercolour, 24 x 19 (61 x 48.3)
   Inscribed 'David Jones 1928'
   Barbara, Countess of Moray

A view almost coterminous with the right edge of no. 51.

53 MONTES ET OMNES COLLES 1928
   Pencil, watercolour and bodycolour,
   19¾ x 24½ (50.2 x 62.2)
   Inscribed 'David Jones '28'
   Whitworth Art Gallery,
   University of Manchester

The title derives from Psalm 148, 'Praise ye the Lord ... mountains and all hills'.

54 ROMAN LAND 1928
   Pencil, watercolour and bodycolour,
   25¾ x 20 (65.4 x 50.8)
   Inscribed 'David Jones '28'
   Lit: P. Hills in *Agenda*, Rhythm Issue, p.136
   National Museum of Wales, Cardiff

Jones recorded on tape for the British Council: 'Roman Land' was also made just outside Lourdes, but looking in the opposite direction (to 'Montes et Omnes Colles'), where there was a Napoleonic cavalry barracks in the distance, which I think was at that date used by some order of nuns. The plough team drawn by oxen, which I don't think I'd seen before, seemed to sum up the whole feeling of France as part of the *Imperium*, and that is why it is called 'Roman Land'.

55 ST JOHN'S WOOD 1928
   Pencil and watercolour, 23 x 16¾ (58.4 x 42.5)
   Inscribed 'David Jones '28'
   Museum of London

A rare example of a street scene, painted soon after Jones's return from France. The liveliness of Bonnard's colour is combined with the childlike vision cultivated by his fellow-members of the Seven and Five Society.

54

[88]

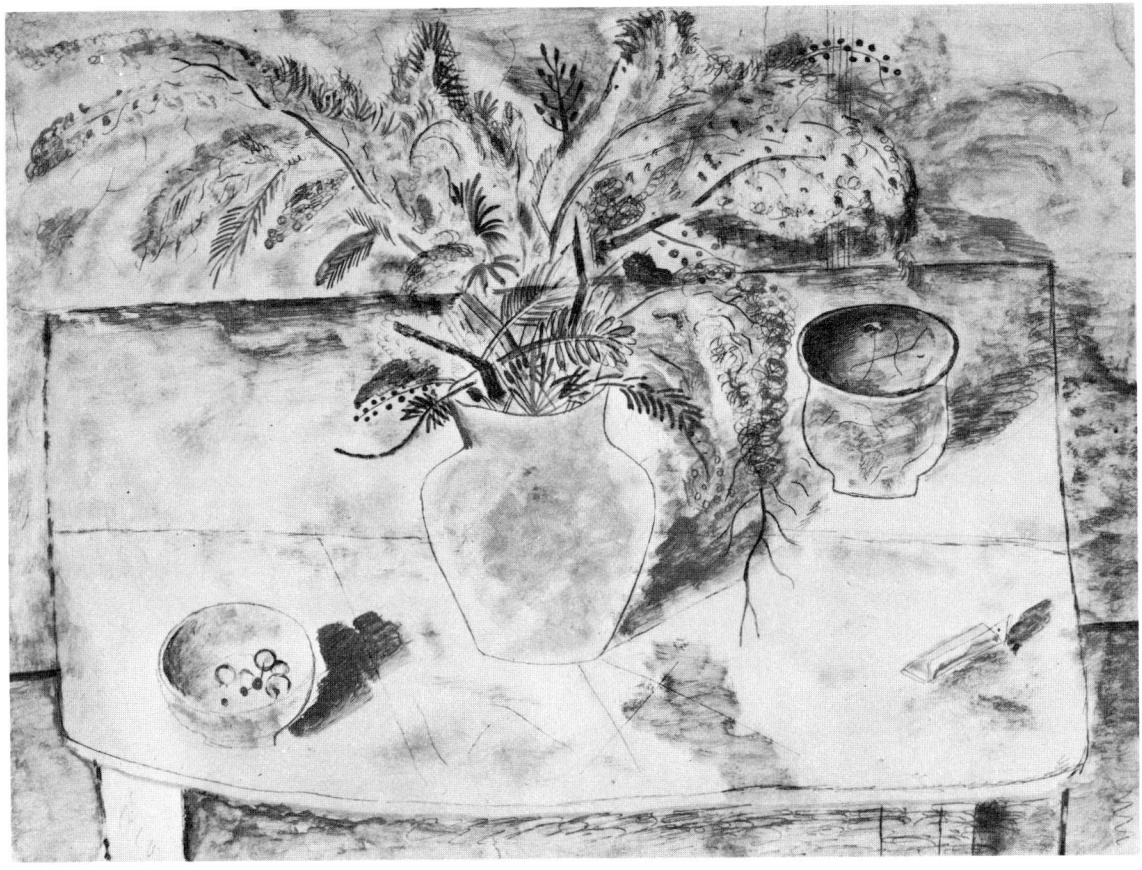

56

56 THE TABLE TOP 1928
Pencil and watercolour, $17\frac{7}{8}$ x $22\frac{3}{4}$ (45.4 x 57.8)
Inscribed 'David Jones '28'
Victoria and Albert Museum

Jones's closest approach to the formal values of Ben Nicholson's early work: see introduction pp.35–6. The tracks of the brush indicate the use of hog-hair as well as traditional soft watercolour brushes. It is not surprising that he should have marked approvingly the following passage in W. J. Muckley, *A Handbook for Painters and Art Students*, London 1882 (2nd ed.) p.109: 'The ordinary sable and hog-hair brushes used for oil-painting are very well suited for watercolour'. (Copy in the National Library of Wales, Aberystwyth.)

57 THE ENGRAVER'S WORKSHOP 1929
Pencil and watercolour, $22\frac{3}{4}$ x $16\frac{3}{8}$ (57.8 x 41.6)
Inscribed 'David Jones 1929'
Private collection

A wide-angle view of the artist's room in his parent's house at Brockley. On the left is the press he used to print his engravings; the tools of the trade, burin and pinchers (for holding the plates while they are warmed over the gas-light) are laid out with care. Behind the press appears to be a map of Wales – or is it a painting? Much to his mother's annoyance, Jones liked to keep the floorboards bare as they reminded him of a ship's decking – and hence of the sacred wood of 'Keel, Ram and Stauros' (see introduction pp.46–7). The pallor of the blazing fire indicates that the reds have faded.

DRAWINGS & PAINTINGS

58 FEMALE NUDE 1929
    Pencil and watercolour, 24¼ x 17½ (61.6 x 44.5)
    Inscribed 'David Jones '29'
    Douglas Cleverdon

The model was drawn at Pigotts by Eric Gill, Oliver Lodge and David Jones. The artist would not permit this rare life-drawing to be exhibited during his lifetime.

59 STILL-LIFE WITH MARTINI BOTTLE c.1929
    Pencil and watercolour, 19¼ x 24½ (48.9 x 62.2)
    Inscribed 'David Jones'
    Private collection

Not precisely datable, but unlikely to be more than a year later than 'The Table Top' of 1928 (no.56).

60 THE TERRACE 1929
    Pencil and watercolour, 25 x 19¼ (63.5 x 48.9)
    Inscribed 'David Jones '29'
    Lit: P. Hills, *The Malahat Review*, 1973, pp.47-8
    Tate Gallery

See introduction pp.46-7. Painted from the same house as nos. 46, 80. In these years he sometimes visited the Tate Gallery with the young Kenneth Clark to look at Turner. There is no doubt that Turner was often in his mind when he painted at Brighton. Later he noted:
'Ruskin, writing of Turner's treatment of the sea, says that however calm the sea he painted he always remembered that same sea heavy and full of discontent under storm. That is half the secret, more than half, of good painting, of good art. Great painting triumphs ... because it has every sort of undertone and overtone, both of form and content, it is both peace *and* war; it must make the lion lie by the lamb *without anyone noticing*, it must hint at December snow, when summer's heat is in the text. In painting a persistent "desire and pursuit of the whole" is needed.'
(*Dying Gaul*, p.141)

*61 JULY CHANGE 1929
     Pencil and watercolour, 23⅝ x 19¼ (60 x 49)
     Inscribed 'David Jones '29'
     Private collection

One of Jones's earliest views of Pigotts, the farmhouse in Buckinghamshire to which Eric Gill moved in

57

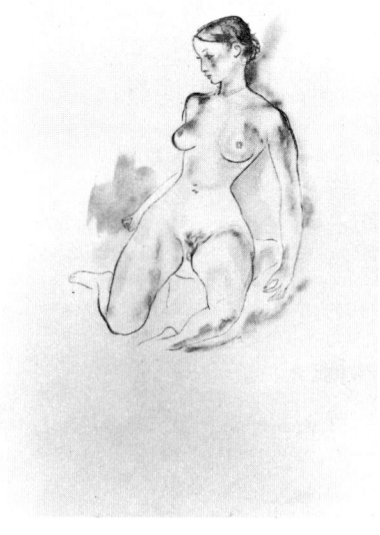

58

DRAWINGS & PAINTINGS

60

62

1928. The colour of Bonnard is wedded to the linearity of the British tradition with new vitality and assurance. The title reveals Jones's love of movement, change, transmogrification.

62 TYWYSOG CARIAD c.1929
    Pencil and watercolour, 12¼ x 9¾ (31.1 x 24.8)
    Inscribed on the Cross BRENHNV CARIAD
    Anthony d'Offay

Reproduced in Agenda 'David Jones Special Issue', 1967, with a caption (probably written by the artist): 'Tywysog Cariad. c.1929. London. Unfinished study for proposed work illustrating the Oblation and Immolation of the Cross and of the Altar in a Welsh hill-setting.' Jones was often erroneous in his retrospective dating; the style of this drawing appears to be close to works of the late 1930s but a date of c.1929 is probable on the basis of comparisons with 'The Bride' and 'Wounded Knight' (nos.15, 16). Tywysog Cariad and Brenhynu Cariad are Welsh for 'Prince of Love' and 'King of Love'. This drawing must be one of Jones's first statements of the inseparable nature of the Crucifixion and the Eucharist, a theme later taken up in his poem The Fatigue,

> where the stripped mensa
>   is set up
>   where the long lancea
>   obliquely thrust
> must drain the Cup
>   for here
>   is immolatio oblata.

(The Sleeping Lord, p.36) The living Christ, reigning from the Tree, is the central image of the Anglo-Saxon poem The Dream of the Rood, of which he wrote in a letter of 1942, 'It's glorious . . . when the Cross speaks about the *weight* of the hero and how the hero and the wood were bound together. It is a loss that this great northern conception of the crucifixion has never *really* been expressed in plastic art.' (Dai Greatcoat, p.122). Lines from The Dream of the Rood were painted in the inscription no. 150.

63 LYNX 1929
    Pencil and watercolour, 13 x 13½ (33 x 34.3)
    Inscribed 'Lynx, David Jones '29'
    Newport Museum and Art Gallery, Gwent

Members of the cat family were the favourite subject at London Zoo.

[91]

DRAWINGS & PAINTINGS

64 SIPHON AND SILVER 1930
    Oil on board, 19¾ x 27 (50.1 x 68.6)
    Inscribed 'David J '30'
    The late N.B.C. Lucas

As in most of Jones's oils, the paint has been so thinned with turpentine that the white preparation of the board shows through. In this way the ground functions as a source of luminosity like the paper in his watercolours, but in both media he preferred to use slightly opaque pigments rather than glazes.

65 ERIC GILL 1930
    Pencil and watercolour, 24 x 19 (61 x 48.2)
    Inscribed 'David Jones '30'
    National Museum of Wales, Cardiff

Jones said of Gill (1882–1940) in a letter to Denis Tegetmeier, 13.xi.'53, 'I still think of him as a kind of Socrates'. That Socratic quality is powerfully felt in this drawing of the stone-carver and letterer in his room at Pigotts. The mysterious presence of the figure is achieved with a minimum of tonal modelling so that there is no divorce between mass and space, solid and void. The colour is not added as decoration but with great economy, gives depth and movement to the space.

66 RENE HAGUE'S PRESS 1930
    Watercolour, 25 x 19 (63.5 x 48.2)
    Inscribed 'David Jones '30'
    Helen Sutherland Collection

A Cope's Albion hand-press on which the first proofs of In Parenthesis were pulled at Pigotts. Whereas Ben Nicholson's ideal was the calm of Piero della Francesca, Jones admired the energy of Celtic ornament, of El Greco and Rubens, Hogarth and Boucher. This watercolour is baroque in its vitality. The claw feet of the press are painted with such animation that they seem to recover their animal life – just one of the innocent metamorphoses of Jones's brush. A colour reproduction appears in Helen Sutherland Collection, Catalogue of the Arts Council Exhibition, London 1970. A darker version of the same subject was exhibited at the Anthony d'Offay Gallery in 1975. On René Hague see no. 91.

67 LADY PRUDENCE PELHAM 1930
    Pencil and watercolour, 23¼ x 18 (59 x 45.7)
    Inscribed 'David J '30'
    T.F. Burns

Jones met Prudence Pelham, the daughter of the sixth Earl of Chichester, when she was staying with the Gills at Pigotts in 1929–30. It was there that a friendship began which René Hague described as 'the most important personal relationship in David's life'. Reference should be made to Dai Greatcoat for some account of the character of 'that lovely rebel' (Hague). She subsequently married Guy Branch, and after his death, Robert Buhler. She died in 1952.

*68 CATH GARTREF 1930
    Pencil and watercolour, 24 x 19 (61 x 48.2)
    Inscribed 'David J '30'
    Miss M.L. Graham

The repetition of the springy curves of the cat throughout the composition is a perfect pictorial metaphor for the spell a cat casts upon its territory. The title, 'cat's home' in Welsh, tells all. From 1930 interior and exterior become ever more interwoven.

69 PIGOTTS FARMYARD 1930
    Pencil, watercolour and bodycolour,
    19¼ x 24⅞ (49 x 63.2)
    Inscribed 'David J '30'
    Peter Guy

David Kindersley describes the scene of this watercolour in The Life and Works of Eric Gill, Los Angeles 1968, p.57:
'Mr Gill's workshops at Pigotts, amongst the beech woods of Buckinghamshire, were converted from fine eighteenth century barns surrounding the farmyard where originally all natural things had been perpetrated. Now as if in honour of the pig, a sty was finely built of brick in the centre of the yard, and his muck hummed and enriched the air – a little too much on a hot day. Mr Gill had his workshop and drawing office on the opposite side to us. At one end were the house and cottages. At the other, the Hague and Gill "press" operated in a long, low outhouse.'
The motif of curtains flying out of windows, which becomes common from this date, may indicate familiarity with the paintings of Stanley Spencer.

65

DRAWINGS & PAINTINGS

*70 PIGOTTS FARM 1930
Pencil and watercolour, 19½ x 25 (49.5 x 63.5)
Inscribed 'David J '30'
Catherine Dupré

Like no. 69, a view from an upstairs window onto the yard at Pigotts. The darks – always crucial in Jones's paintings – signal and hold with precision in a turbulent sea of colour.

71 FLOWERS AND TEACUP 1930
Pencil and watercolour, 24 x 18¾ (61 x 47.6)
Inscribed 'David Jones '30'
Private collection

72 THOMAS HODGKIN 1930
Pencil and watercolour, 24 x 19¼ (61 x 49)
Inscribed 'David J. '30'
Thomas Hodgkin

Thomas Hodgkin writes, 'I was wearing David Jones's jacket and scarf – which he put on me as I had just come in from playing tennis. The painting was done in David's usual little room over the porch at Rock Hall – in August 1930, I would think.' The portrait was finished at the one sitting. Jones tended to fall back on a stock motif for the hands, and uncertainty in this foreground area mars many of his otherwise incisive portraits.

73 AGNES FOUNTAIN 1930
Watercolour, 22¼ x 30¼ (56.5 x 76.8)
Inscribed 'David '30'
Helen Sutherland Collection

Probably painted at Rock Hall; the reason for the title is uncertain. It may refer to Agno, a nymph whom Pausanias tells us gave her name to a fountain on mount Lycaeus. When the priest of Jupiter, after a prayer, stirred the waters of this fountain with a bough, a thick vapour arose, which was soon dissolved into a plentiful shower. The watercolour was included in the Seven and Five Society exhibition in January 1931.

74 MERLIN APPEARS IN THE FORM OF A
YOUNG CHILD TO ARTHUR
SLEEPING 1930
Pencil and monochrome bodycolour,
10½ x 8 (26.7 x 20.3)
Michael Richey

67

69

Reproduced in *The Anathemata* as 'Merlin-land' and dated 1931. David Blamires (*David Jones: Artist and Writer*, p.65) writes, 'The theme of the picture is derived from Malory's *Tale of King Arthur* (I, 19f.), where Arthur has fallen asleep after the departure of the Questing Beast and Merlin appears to him "lyke a chylde of fourtene yere of ayge" and informs him of his extraordinary parentage, thus making him aware of both his heritage and his calling.' It may not be accidental that Arthur's pose recalls the Man of Sorrows.

DRAWINGS & PAINTINGS

75

75 OLD ANIMAL FROM TIBET 1930
Pencil and watercolour, 15¾ x 18¾ (40 x 47.6)
Inscribed 'David J 30'
National Museum of Wales, Cardiff

A yak, drawn in Regent's Park zoo. Jones said of the zoo drawings, 'I used pencil and watercolour, as it were, at the same time. I mean, I didn't draw and then use colour: the colour was an integral part of the work.' (British Council tape recording, edited by Peter Orr.)

76 JAGUAR 1931
Pencil and watercolour, 12½ x 18½ (31.7 x 47)
Inscribed 'David Jones '31'
The Cooper Art Collection by permission of the Trustees in conjunction with South Yorkshire County Council, The Cooper Gallery, Barnsley

One of Jones's finest studies of an animal moving.

77 PANTHERS IN REGENT'S PARK ZOO 1931
Pencil and watercolour, 12½ x 21 (31.7 x 53.3)
Inscribed 'David Jones '31'
Walker Art Gallery, Liverpool

[95]

DRAWINGS & PAINTINGS

78 HUMAN BEING 1931
Oil on canvas, 29½ x 23¾ (75 x 60.3)
Inscribed 'David J. '31'
Lit: *Word and Image*, no.75
Helen Sutherland Collection

Described as a 'quasi self-portrait'. The quality of this oil, particularly the sombre richness of browns and maroons, shows that the lessons of Sickert had not been forgotten. The interplay between firmly delineated shapes, such as the ear and neck, and loosely painted quasi-abstract mottling was typical of Seven and Five painting at this time. 'Human Being' was hung in the Seven and Five exhibition in February 1932.

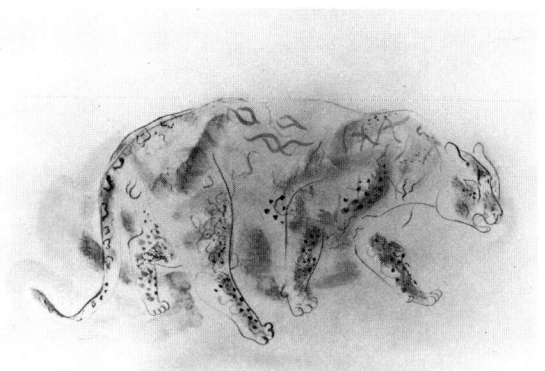

76

*79 PLACE FOR SHIPS 1931
Pencil and watercolour, 19¼ x 25¼ (49 x 64.1)
Inscribed 'David Jones 1931'
Richard Smart

The house rented by Jones's parents at Portslade (see no. 46) flanked, on the western side, a small harbour. To an artist whose grandfather had been a mast-and-block maker, and whose mind was steeped in the Ancient Mariner, the *activity* as much as the picturesqueness of a place for ships attracted attention. Though loading and unloading, furbishing and refitting, is not literally described, the liveliness of design acts as pictorial metaphor for such activity. In the details of the watercolour the same imagination is discernible that asked in the 'Redriff' section of *The Anathemata* (p.118),

Did he bespeak

of Eb Bradshaw, Princes Stair:
listed replacement of sheaves to the running-
blocks, new dead-eyes to the standing shrouds,
some spare hearts for the stays, a heavy repair in
the chains, some nice work up at the hound ...

*80 MANAWYDAN'S GLASS DOOR 1931
Watercolour, 25 x 19⅜ (63.5 x 49.2)
Lit: D. Blamires, p.56; Arthur Giardelli, *Agenda*, David Jones Special Issue, 1973/4, pp.90–8
Arthur Giardelli

Arthur Giardelli writes:
'Does the title matter? What is Manawydan to us? The clue can be followed in Lady Charlotte Guest's translation of the *Mabinogion* where David Jones first

78

DRAWINGS & PAINTINGS

read of Manawydan. What is recalled in this painting is told in the second of the Four Branches of the Mabinogi entitled "Branwen the daughter of Llyr". "Bendigeid Vran, the son of Llyr, was the crowned king of this island and he was exalted from the crown of London." He is killed in a war in Ireland but, before he dies, he commands Manawydan and Pryderi that they shall take his head and bury it under the White Mount in London where it shall ensure that no invaders shall plague the island. It is when they are on their way to London with the head that they pass fourscore years in a royal hall in Gwales. The door in the picture was that of which Manawydan says, "See, yonder, is the door we may not open". So long as they do not open it they remain oblivious of every sorrow and loss and unaware of the passage of time. It was from behind this very door in Hove that David Jones had escaped from time in making many works. Here he started writing In Parenthesis.'

81 FACTORY COAST 1931
    Oil on panel, 20 x 24 (50.8 x 61)
    Inscribed 'David J '31' and on the verso
    'May 1931'
    Helen Sutherland Collection

There appears to be no record as to where this was painted. He was definitely at Portslade in late April, so it is possible that 'Factory Coast' was painted on the south coast to the east of there the following month.

82 ISABELLA DRUMMOND 1931
    Pencil and watercolour, $23\frac{3}{4}$ x $19\frac{1}{8}$ (60.5 x 48.5)
    Inscribed 'David J '31'
    Professor C. J. Hamson

This portrait was drawn at Pigotts in July. Isabella Drummond married Charles John Hamson in 1933. Beneath the Celtic embroidery of flowers there is a classic sense of form. Later Jones jotted in the margin of The Decline of the West a criticism of Spengler's opposition of classic form and 'Faustian' space: 'The trouble with this otherwise accurate theory as to the antithesis of the Classic and the Faustian, is that actually there is vast space in good Classic art. There is "distance" round limbs and torsos as "immaterial" as that in the paintings of the masters of the West . . . and if one tries to copy a good Classic nude figure one finds this out – the circumference of a thigh is somehow made as extensive as a landscape & the difference between original and "copy" is usually in this, the "copy" loses that extension and space sense.' (Copy in the National Library of Wales, Aberystwyth.)

*83 PETRA IM ROSENHAG 1931
     Pencil, watercolour and bodycolour,
     30 x 22 (76.2 x 56)
     Inscribed 'David J '31'
     Lord Clark

Petra, Eric Gill's second daughter, had been engaged to David Jones between 1923 and 1926. This portrait was drawn at Pigotts the year after her marriage to Denis Tegetmeier. The sittings rarely lasted more than half an hour, and the watercolour was completed in about a month. It was submitted to the Goupil Salon in September 1931.

The appellation im Rosenhag alludes to Northern Renaissance paintings of the Madonna in a rose arbour. Jones may have had in mind Martin Schongauer's Madonna at Colmar; he certainly admired the masterly line of Schongauer's engravings. But the most obvious allusion is to the goddess Flora of Botticelli's 'Primavera'. The flowers that issue from the mouth of the earth nymph Gaia, in the 'Primavera', blossom into the fullness of Flora, the embodiment of the fertility of spring. As with Flora, so also with Petra, the flowers of the arbour and the flowers of her dress are magically confused, and the flowers upon the table tattoo her arm with the embroidery of the hedgerows of Britain – just as they embroider the doublet and hose of the courtiers in Nicholas Hilliard's miniatures. Flora strews roses from her lap, Petra holds a kerchief in her lap – with which she would seem to catch the falling blossoms and offer them towards us.

There can be no doubt that 'Petra im Rosenhag' is also the Celtic Blodeuedd of the Mabinogion, described in The Anathemata as 'the woman made by enchantment out of oak-flower, meadowsweet and broom-flower in the tale of Math son of Mathonwy' (p.152, n.5). More than an individual portrait, the picture celebrates woman as source of fruitfulness and as protectress. A clue to its solemnity can be found on page 191 of The Anathemata where the arbour of the Madonna is associated with the arbor – the wood – of the Cross:

DRAWINGS & PAINTINGS

You who decked *die Blumendame* and our Blodeuedd formed.
      Lovely Flora
how variant you are.
      You can tendril and galloon
chose queens, im *Rosenhage*
had you no hand in
     this arbour
      too?

84 ARCHWAY AT PIGOTTS c.1931
   Pencil and watercolour, $25\frac{1}{8}$ x $19\frac{1}{2}$ (63.8 x 49.5)
   Nicolete Gray

85 TRADE SHIP PASSES YNYS BYR 1931
   Watercolour and bodycolour,
   $18\frac{3}{4}$ x $23\frac{3}{4}$ (47.6 x 60.3)
   Inscribed 'David Jones '31'
   Private collection

Ynys Byr is the Welsh name for Caldy. Jones painted some of his most fluid seascapes there when he revisited the island in October 1931. Pencil is virtually abandoned in favour of drawing directly with the tip of the brush. The rocks are brightly patterned with Celtic interlace of many colours. The chameleon hues of sea and wet sand recall the lines of The *Anathemata* (p.95),
And now his celestial influence gains:
     across the atmosphere
     on the water-sphere
and the wide sinus changes humour and the sea-hues suffer change . . .

86 THE REEFED PLACE 1931
   Watercolour and bodycolour,
   24 x $18\frac{7}{8}$ (61 x 48)
   Inscribed 'David J '31'
   Private collection

Painted at Caldy; see no. 85.

86

87 THE CHAPEL PERILOUS 1932
   Pencil and watercolour, 19 x 24 (48.2 x 61)
   Inscribed 'David J '32'
   Helen Sutherland Collection

Nicolete Gray describes the setting of Helen Sutherland's house, Rock Hall:
'The garden was beautiful too with a wide lawn going down to a lake, and beyond a wood, and at

DRAWINGS & PAINTINGS

the back beyond the walled garden one came to the
great double or triple avenue of trees, planted in
1820, stretching for over a mile, from the house all
the way to the Great North Road. One used to go for
walks in the avenue after dinner, in the dusk, or by
moonlight, hearing the hooting of the owls ....
Just beyond the garden, almost in the drive, was
the tiny village of Rock, a row of pretty stone
cottages; opposite them the church which is
Norman, very small too. The village, the church,
the lake and the wood are all in David Jones's
painting "The Chapel Perilous". You could see them
out of the window of the room which he always
used to have, above the front door in the original
tower.'
(*Helen Sutherland Collection*, Catalogue of the Arts Council
Exhibition, London 1970, pp.17–18)

87

Malory's *Morte Darthur* was much in Jones's mind
while he was staying at Rock; Bamburgh Castle,
which was reputed to be the Joyous Garde to which
Launcelot took the queen, was not far away. He
associated the church and churchyard at Rock with
the description of Launcelot's arrival at the Chapel
Perilous in Book VI, Chapter 15. The same passage is
alluded to in *In Parenthesis* (p.31) and it seems that
Mametz Wood, the perilous wood in which Jones
was wounded in 1916, was also compounded in his
imagination with this Northumberland wood.

91

*88   THE QUEEN'S DISH 1932
      Watercolour, 22 x 30¼ (55.8 x 76.8)
      Inscribed 'David Jones '32'
      The late N.B.C. Lucas

The Queen of the title may be Guenever; for sugges-
tions about the Grail symbolism see the introduction
pp.50–5. Jones referred to this in conversation as
'one of my best'; he might have had it in mind
when he wrote, in the 1940s,
'Though the dealer's clumsy title is: "Still Life with
Dessert", yet, if the forms are so contrived, it *may* be
that some of the "content" of the Tellus* on the
Ara Pacis Augustae, the fruits and grain stalks, the gifts
of the Augustan Peace depicted on that monument
to concluded war in the West, will get into that
apple on the dish, and into the bunch of flowers – if
the artist is a sufficiently subtle master of whatever
is meant by *recta ratio factibilium* – and all which that
may imply with regard to the art of painting, and

[100]

if, further, he has Tellus for his mother, or at least has sucked a little at her breast, and has not altogether disowned her. For remember, what is signified must be always much the same, whatever the diversity of means. It is always Leda and always the Swan. It is always this "admirable commerce" which is the "subject" of art.
*Tellus Mater, the deity of Mother-Earth; honoured together with Ceres as the goddess of fruitfulness, she was both womb and grave.'
(Dying Gaul, pp.141–2)

89   CATTLE IN THE PARK 1932
Watercolour and bodycolour,
$23\frac{1}{2}$ x 18 (59.7 x 45.7)
Inscribed 'David J '32'
Trustees of the late Mrs F.H. Low

Painted from a window at Rock.

90   THE LONG MEADOW 1932
Pencil and watercolour, 22 x $33\frac{3}{8}$ (55.9 x 84.8)
Inscribed 'David J '32'
Douglas Cleverdon

Drawn from the house at Pigotts.

91   THE TRANSLATOR OF THE CHANSON
DE ROLAND (René Gabriel Hague) 1932
Pencil and watercolour, $30\frac{1}{2}$ x 22 (77.5 x 55.8)
Inscribed 'David Jones '32'
National Museum of Wales, Cardiff

René Hague (1905–81) married Eric Gill's eldest daughter Joan in 1930. 'A hand-press (see no. 66) was installed at Pigotts and René became a master of the craft. Small books in limited editions followed one another and each had the touch of genius in the spacing of type and the sense of proportion. What little leisure there was in this cottage industry went into the making of scholarly translations like The Song of Roland, and René made the art of translation peculiarly his own.... René has a great sensitivity for language, a relationship to it like that of James Joyce. Physically and mentally he was ever reminiscent of that man.' (Tom Burns in The Tablet, 31 January 1981) In the last years of his life Hague wrote a general study of David Jones and a commentary on The Anathemata, as well as editing Dai Greatcoat: A self-portrait of David Jones in his letters. Written with erudition and wit, these books were the fruit of half a century of the closest friendship. No one has contributed so much to our understanding of David Jones and his work.

Jones's drawing successfully captures the alert intelligence and darting wit of his friend. Around the marble firmness of the slender neck all is in movement. The colours – pale greens and yellows balancing maroons and chestnuts – recede and advance, counterpointing the movement of line in space.

92   THE VIOLIN 1932
Watercolour, $22\frac{1}{2}$ x 31 (57.1 x 78.7)
Inscribed 'David Jones '32'
Victoria and Albert Museum

*93   BRIAR CUP 1932
Pencil and watercolour, $30\frac{1}{8}$ x $21\frac{3}{4}$ (76.5 x 55.2)
Inscribed 'David J '32'
Helen Sutherland Collection

'David Jones's inner eye, upon which Celtic traditional stories have had their effect, looks outward with "an affection for the intimate creatureliness of things ... an appreciation of the particular genius of places, men, trees, animals", and, let it be added, of scissors, razor blades, tooth brushes, window catches; his sympathy with such minutiae has been given profuse expression in the pulsating details of "English Window", "Curtained Outlook" (no. 97) and "Briar Cup". It is a sympathy so lively that, settling upon inanimate objects, it seems to animate, and even, as legends will, to humanize them. Such an anthropomorphic perceptiveness could not but lead his imagination onward to a vision of things as being able almost to melt from one species into another, "a pervading sense of metamorphosis and mutability" in the world.'
(Robin Ironside, David Jones, p.14)

94   THORN CUP 1932
Pencil and watercolour, 22 x 30 (56 x 76.2)
Inscribed 'David Jones '32'
Mr and Mrs Christopher Hull

For possible Grail symbolism, see introduction p.55. The dish propped upright on the window-sill may allude to the paten, the plate for the bread in the

Mass. On seeing the watercolour again, in 1969, Jones described it as 'bloody, bold and resolute', and indeed it appears to have been drawn with a kind of furious concentration.

95 THE LINEN CLOTH 1932
    Pencil and watercolour, 30 x 22 (76.2 x 56)
    Inscribed 'David Jones '32 Sept.'
    Sir Antony Hornby

Although ostensibly a still-life it may be that even here, in this linen cloth with the air buoying it up, Jones perceived a reminder of an altar. Later he was to write of the moment in the Mass when the priest kisses the altar-cloth,

> lightly & swiftly his lips
> press, in medio, the uppermost of the
> three-fold, fine abbed fair cloths
>   of Eblana flax
> that must pall
>   the mensa Domini
> these are indeed 'his own raiment.'
> (*Kensington Mass*, p.9)

96 PETRA 1932
    Pencil and watercolour, 30¾ x 22 (77.2 x 56)
    Inscribed 'David J '32'
    Helen Sutherland Collection

In a list of the pictures for reproduction in Robin Ironside's *David Jones* the artist entitled this 'The Seated Mother, Autumn 1932'. The sculptural command of this drawing of Petra Tegetmeier indicates that Jones was about to explore new territory when illness struck in late 1932. Unlike in his earlier portraits, the hands and arms are now integral to the turning of the form in space. Barbara Hepworth and Henry Moore had been elected to the Seven and Five Society in 1931; Jones's new assurance reflects his closer acquaintance with their work – for example Moore's the 'Half-figure of a girl' (Tate Gallery), shown at the Seven and Five exhibition in February 1932.

97 CURTAINED OUTLOOK 1932
    Pencil and watercolour, 30⅝ x 21¾ (77.8 x 55.7)
    British Council

See no. 93, and introduction p.57. Drawn at Pigotts. In 1943 the artist looked back on these works of 1932:

'Very likely I should never have developed any of

97

DRAWINGS & PAINTINGS

99

100

such life as exists in the 1930 period but for a combination of accidents, both in life and thought – and the depth of badness as an artist of which I am capable is easily proved by a glance at earlier work – and that much earlier thing I got from old Hartrick was only usable after I had been through the Eric thing.... I'm sure it's a point chaps don't see – it's a long up and down process, at least with blokes like me. The only thing I know (or think I know) for certain is that what I want a painting to be did become clear, in direction, up at Capel and on Caldy, and that the 1932 group got nearest to what I had in mind – but a very long way from the goal. (I suppose that may partly explain my complete crash – I was conscious for some time before it came that I was straining every nerve to do something more than I had power to do.)' (Dai Greatcoat, p.124)

98   WINDOW AT ROCK 1936
     Pencil and watercolour, $24\frac{3}{4}$ x $19\frac{1}{4}$ (63 x 49)
     Inscribed 'David J '36'
     Helen Sutherland Collection

This view at Helen Sutherland's house was Jones's first successful drawing after four years of nervous illness.

99   FRONTISPIECE TO 'IN PARENTHESIS' 1937
     Pencil, ink and watercolour, 15 x 11 (38.1 x 28)
     Inscribed 'David J. '37'
     Lit: R. L. Charles in Amgueddfa, p.7
     National Museum of Wales, Cardiff

See introduction pp.58–9; in addition to the associations noted in the introduction, it may be that Jones had in mind the opening of The Pilgrim's Progress: 'I saw a man clothed in rags (Isa. lxiv:6.), standing in a certain place, ... and a great burden upon his back'. Paul Fussell draws attention to the many references to Bunyan amongst writers of The Great War (The Great War and Modern Memory, Oxford 1975, pp.137–44).

100 TAILPIECE TO 'IN PARENTHESIS':
     THE VICTIM 1937
     Pencil, ink and watercolour, 15 x 11 (38.1 x 28)
     Inscribed 'David J.'
     National Museum of Wales, Cardiff

See introduction pp.58–9. This drawing and the Frontispiece were conceived as designs for engravings.

[103]

'The artist wrote beneath it, and later rubbed out, the Latin words of the verse in Revelation "I beheld and lo . . . stood a lamb as it had been slain".' (R.L. Charles, *Amgueddfa*, p.7). Like all David Jones's signs, the image of the soldier as sacrificial Lamb was not without origin in things seen and touched: 'Short jackets made from the hide of sheep or goats or other beasts, were issued to the troops in the line against the cold. They were afterwards abandoned in favour of dressed leather ones, which, though far less fascinating, were less an abode for lice.' (*In Parenthesis*, Part 2, note 3) When, as on occasions, the sheepskins were worn with the fleece outermost, the metamorphosis was complete (c.f. Fussell, *Great War*, pp. 239–43).

101 LLYS CEIMIAD: LA BASSEE FRONT, 1916
    1937
    Pencil, ink and watercolour,
    15 x 12½ (38.1 x 31.7)
    National Library of Wales, Aberystwyth

In 1972 the artist explained:
'Ceimiad means "champion" or "hero", and "Llys" the court or place of importance. In the Middle Ages the residence of a prince was a *llys*. So the title here means only that for the front-fighters (as old Jerry called the trench soldiers) a dug-out of some sort was a *llys*. I say on *la Bassée front* because I had in mind a particular bit of line round about Givenchy, where the forward trenches were very meandering, and not so flat as in some sectors, so that you could see chaps in the next firebay; and the enemy line front was pretty close, very comfortless and untidy, saturated with damp and broken revetment wire. Trench drain beneath the duck-boards filled with water, the somewhat makeshift "cubby-holes" contrived in the side of the earth, the parados.

The chaps with their feet bare, stretching out of the dug-out, were breaking a very strict rule, for one was very rightly forbidden to take one's boots off in the front line, for obvious reasons – I remember doing so once with unfortunate consequences, for quite unexpectedly the enemy decided to shell the place very heavily, in the pitch dark, and of course I could not find my left boot in time to get out of the place – but eventually did, and it was a nightmare while it lasted. Never again! Whatever else you took off – keep yr boots on!' (*Word and Image*, no. 91, p. 50)

*102 THE FARM DOOR 1937
    Pencil and watercolour, 28¾ x 20 (73 x 50.8)
    Inscribed 'David Jones'
    Private collection

1937 is written on the back of the frame in the artist's handwriting. In a letter of 1944 he listed it as 'Door of little room at Pigotts with cattle outside, and flowers etc'. (*Dai Greatcoat*, p.127) This vigorous drawing brings together in unique juxtaposition two of Jones's favourite subjects, animals and flowers. The new spareness of colour – notice the quivering hues in the penumbra behind the door – characterises his drawings from this date onwards.

The year after 'The Farm Door' was painted, Jones wrote about the relationship between his drawing and the illness that had plagued him since 1933: 'It still seems to tend to bring back my stuff more than other things, and consequently it is a very wearisome and slow job doing a bit when I can, and making not much headway, and I only know one way to draw and that is in a kind of fierce concentration.

The only times a drawing is good is when you nearly break yourself turning the corner from a muddle into a clarity, and it takes every ounce of nervous effort to be any good – so it is very difficult to proceed gingerly and soberly and stop when you know it will be probably fatal (I mean fatal because of bringing on some bloody recurrence of nerves) to go on and hope to recapture something next time . . .'
(Letter of 14 February 1938, *Dai Greatcoat*, p.83)

103 PAUL TAKING BREAD IN THE BOAT 1937
    Pencil, 8¼ x 6½ (21 x 16.5)
    Lit: *Word and Image*, no.92
    Michael Richey

Drawn while Jones was living in the Fort Hotel in Sidmouth, Devon. The relative simplicity of the line is due to the fact that it was made as a design for Gill to engrave. The drawing refers, in unusually explicit terms, to the image of the ship as the Church (*navis*=nave). St Paul, marked with the stigmata, blesses five loaves and two fishes, while being taken under arrest from Caesarea to Rome in the ship that is wrecked off Malta. The boy, holding a candle in one hand and Paul's planeta in the other, confirms the eucharistic nature of the meal. The identification of the priest at Mass with the sacrifice of the

DRAWINGS & PAINTINGS

104

Redeemer on the Cross is indicated by the 'disguised symbolism' of placing Paul before the mast and cross-bar.

104 THE CRICKET MATCH, SIDMOUTH 1937
     Pencil and watercolour, 19 x 24 (48.2 x 61)
     Inscribed 'David Jones '37'
     Mrs Francis d'Abreu

In the mid 1930s Jones was entertained by reading the novels of Trollope, and this drawing from a window of the Fort Hotel has an almost Trollopean sense of comedy.

105 ESCAPING FIGURE CARRYING
     TRINKETS late 1930s
     Pencil, $12\frac{1}{4}$ x $7\frac{1}{2}$ (31.1 x 19)
     Inscribed 'David J'
     Private collection

Jones described this drawing in conversation as 'a Romano-British woman hiding her treasures at the time of the invasions'. It was intended as an illustration to The Anathemata but not used. It probably dates from the late 1930s.

[105]

DRAWINGS & PAINTINGS

106 CHURCH TOWER AT MELLS 1939
Pencil and watercolour, 19 x 24 (48.2 x 61)
Lady Helen Asquith, OBE

In July 1939 Jones stayed with the Asquiths at the Manor House of Mells in Somerset, where this drawing was made from his bedroom window.

107 PROMENADING AT SIDMOUTH 1940
Pencil and watercolour, $19\frac{3}{4}$ x $24\frac{1}{2}$ (50.2 x 62.2)
Inscribed 'David Jones '40'
David and Camilla Bosanquet

A view on a windy day from his bedroom at the Fort Hotel.

107

108 GUENEVER 1940
Pencil, ink and watercolour,
$24\frac{1}{2}$ x $19\frac{1}{2}$ (62.2 x 49.5)
Inscribed 'David Jones 1940'
Lit: *Tate Gallery Catalogue: Modern British paintings, drawings, and sculptures*, I, London 1964, pp.343-5
Tate Gallery

Morte Darthur, Book XIX, ch.6, Launcelot comes to Guenever in the Castle of Sir Meliagraunce. 'Then the knights that were hurt were searched, and soft salves were laid to their wounds; ... Then when season was, they went unto their chambers, but in no wise the queen would not suffer the wounded knights to be from her, but that they were laid within draughts by her chamber, upon beds and pillows, that she herself might see to them that they wanted nothing. So when Sir Launcelot was in his chamber that was assigned to him, he called unto him Sir Lavaine, and told him that he must go to speak with his lady, Dame Guenever.... Then Sir Launcelot took his sword in his hand, and privily went to a place where he had espied a ladder to forehand, and that he took under his arm, and bare it through the garden, and set it up to the window, and there anon the queen was ready to meet him. And then they made either to other their complaints of many diverse things, and then Sir Launcelot wished that he might have come in to her. Wit ye well, said the queen, I would as fain as ye, that ye might come in to me.... Now shall I prove my might, said Sir Launcelot, for your love; and then he set his hands upon the bars of iron, and he pulled at them with such a might that he brast them clene out of the stone walls, and therewithal one of the bars of iron cut the brawn of his hands throughout to the bone; and then he leapt into the chamber of the queen.' (Everyman edition, Vol. II, pp.323-4.)

On Launcelot's love for Guenever as an allegory of that of Christ for the Virgin Mary, see the introduction p.65. The wounded knights that Guenever tends are representative of mankind which, according to Catholic theology, has the crucial benefit of the Virgin's intercession before God. In his drawing Jones makes visual reference to all the ages of the world for whom this intercession is eternally necessary; thus we recognize not only the Crusading knights with legs crossed, but the long-barrow sleepers of prehistory, the soldiers of the First War in their dug-out, and all those who in 1940 had to shelter from the air-raids. The knight on the left (who recalls Mantegna's 'Dead Christ' in the Brera) shows how far the circumstances of the Second World War had led Jones to anticipate the vision of Henry Moore's shelter drawings. Not surprisingly, he later singled out Moore's studies of 1941-3 for special praise (*Dai Greatcoat*, p.191).

DRAWINGS & PAINTINGS

[107]

DRAWINGS & PAINTINGS

109 THE FOUR QUEENS 1941
Pencil, ink and watercolour,
24½ x 19½ (62.2 x 49.5)
Inscribed 'David Jones 1941'
Lit: *Tate Gallery Catalogue: Modern British paintings, drawings, and sculpture*, I, London 1964, p.345; D. Blamires, pp.66–7; P. Hills, *Malahat Review*, pp.59–60
Tate Gallery

See introduction p.65. The subject is from *Morte Darthur*, Book VI, ch.3. 'The Queen of Eastland (with falcon), the Queen of the Out Isles, the Queen of North Wales, and Queen Morgan le Fay contend for the love of Launcelot. Morgan le Fay is casting an enchantment on him as he sleeps. The swan in the water by Launcelot's head suggests Guenever, and Morgan le Fay's spell is countered by his dream thought of her.' (*Word and Image*, no.98, p.51) The landscape is based on Jones's memory of Capel-y-ffin, with the ruined chapel and Y Twmpa (see no.42). The dolmen in the distance on the left and the horses incised on the hills are reminders of the antiquity of these 'colles Arthuri'.

109

*110 APHRODITE IN AULIS 1941
Pencil, ink and watercolour,
24½ x 19¾ (62.9 x 49.5)
Inscribed 'David Jones '41'
Lit: D. Blamires, pp.67–9; *The Tate Gallery 1976–8: Illustrated Catalogue of Acquisitions*, pp.96–9
Tate Gallery

Inscribed on the verso 'Aphrodite Pandemos: The Triple Goddess', 'Turan' (these alternative titles crossed out) and 'The Lady'. For detailed discussion of this drawing see introduction pp.60–2. Its progress can be charted from letters printed in *Dai Greatcoat*: 30 June 1940, 'I'm doing a picture of Phryne the hetaira and the sum of all beauty, who showed her splendours to the Court (at least her counsel did) and so impressed them that they said she was innocent.' (p.98) 4 September 1940, 'Still trying to do my picture of Phryne – hope it gets done. I've made her into a nice girl – it is an interesting picture to do.' (p.106) 21 June 1941, 'I had completed my picture of "Phryne" and completed the "Four Queens find Launcelot sleeping" . . .' (p.111). Before 1949 no.110 was simply known as 'Aphrodite'; the addition 'in Aulis' was adopted from a suggestion by

112

[108]

Nicolete Gray (see *Tate Catalogue of Acquisitions*, p.98). In a letter to René Hague he later explained why he changed Euripides' 'Iphigeneia in Aulis' to Aphrodite in Aulis:

'My intention in changing Iphigeneia to Aphrodite in the title was to include *all* female cult-figures, as I have written somewhere the figure is all goddesses rolled into one – wounded of necessity as are all things worthy of our worship – she's mother-figure and *virgo inter virgines* – the pierced woman and mother & all her foretypes. She is "Elen the bracelet-giver" of *In Parenthesis* also, & also the many-wounded Mair, Rhiannon of the *Mabinogion, Ceidwades Wen*, mundi Domina, "not a puff of wind without her" in the Lady of the Pool section, p.128. In *The Anathemata*, the Lady of the Pool refers to Our Lady as comprehending in herself all the potent pre-Xtian cult-figures and their sufferings:

> She's as she of Aulis, master:
> not a puff of wind without her!
> her fiat is our fortune, sir; like Helen's face
> t'was that as launched the ship.'
> (Hague, *Commentary*, p.38)

The moon above the goddess's head and the stars in her hair are attributes of the Madonna of the Apocalypse. Though the birds may be the sea-birds appropriate to the shore, no doubt they allude to the doves sacred to Aphrodite; from one a radiance shines down in token of Annunciation. Thus the birds add their chorus to the confusion of sacred and physical love which is the essential theme of this remarkable drawing. In a note for his doctor, written in 1947, Jones described 'Aphrodite' as 'successful and authentic', but added 'considered not psychologically balanced'. (*Dai Greatcoat*, p.138)

111 STUDY FOR APHRODITE IN AULIS 1938–40
Pencil, $12\frac{7}{8}$ x $8\frac{1}{4}$ (32.7 x 21)
Tate Gallery

See no. 110 and introduction p.60–2.

112 TIGER 1941
Pencil, ink and watercolour,
20 x $14\frac{1}{2}$ (50.8 x 36.8)
Private collection

The artist was especially fond of this drawing.

113 EPIPHANY 1941: BRITANNIA AND GERMANIA EMBRACING
Pencil and watercolour, $11\frac{3}{4}$ x $9\frac{1}{4}$ (29.9 x 23.5)
Inscribed 'Sisters Two, what may we do?'
T. F. Burns

See introduction pp.59–60. The Coventry Carol (*Oxford Book of Carols*, no.22), from which the inscription derives, was traditionally associated with the Massacre of the Innocents, hence its appropriateness at a time when the cities of Coventry and Dresden were being bombed. By a rather curious chance, at some time between 1936 and 1938 the emblem of the lighthouse was added to the figure of Britannia on the verso of the penny. There can be little doubt that the lighthouse of 'Epiphany 1941' is at once the sign of Britannia and of the Virgin Mary, the *Stella Maris*, 'Day-star o' the Harbour' (*The Anathemata*, p.195), and T.S. Eliot's 'Lady, whose shrine stands on the promontory' (*The Dry Salvages*, IV).

114 THE MOTHER OF THE WEST c.1942
Pencil, ink and watercolour,
$10\frac{1}{4}$ x 14 (26 x 35.6)
Inscribed 'from David J.' and 'The Mother of the West'
Tyne and Wear County Council Museums
(Laing Art Gallery, Newcastle upon Tyne)

Photographs of this drawing were sent as a Christmas card in about 1942. The Roman wolf, that 'brights Capitoline for ever' (*Sleeping Lord*, p.11), gives suck not to Romulus and Remus but to the *Agnus Dei*. The setting is a beleaguered outpost of the empire, flanking a Roman wall such as Hadrian's. The time is the end of the Roman era when their gods are failing, but the life blood is passed on to Christianity.

The holly around the wolf's neck and the Star of Bethlehem below are fitting for the Christmas season. The candle in the wolf's paw is the *Lumen Christi*, the Paschal candle. The lily beneath the lamb's hoof is a sign that it is immaculate. The eucharistic nature of the lamb is indicated by the monstrance that stands in the foreground and the altar in the apse behind. A fallen plinth, on the left, is inscribed UBI CARITAS ET AMOR DEUS IBI EST, a theme reiterated in the embrace of two soldiers on the right, one with a British helmet, one with a German.

The idea for the setting in this drawing may well have derived from Jones's attentive reading of R.G.

DRAWINGS & PAINTINGS

"O sisters two what may we do Epiphany 1941

114

Collingwood and J.N.L. Myres *Roman Britain and the English Settlements*, Oxford 1936. Explanation is given there as to why St Martin's church at Brampton in Cumberland was built within the walls of a Roman fort: 'for many early Christians, like St Cybi at Holyhead, chose Roman forts for the sites of their churches, whether because they found British communities living there, or in order to emphasize the truth that Christianity was the spiritual heir of the Roman empire.' (p.310) Jones's annotated copy of Collingwood and Myres is in the National Library of Wales, Aberystwyth. Finally, there is no doubt that his experience on the Western Front cannot have been far from his mind when making this drawing (c.f. the description of the shelled church, *In Parenthesis*, p.149).

115 HELEN THE EMPRESS 1944
   Pencil, ink and watercolour, $9\frac{5}{8}$ x $7\frac{1}{2}$ (24.4 x 19)
   Inscribed 'D.J. '44'
   Mrs D. Tegetmeier

Sent as a birthday card to Petra Tegetmeier; inscribed on the verso,
   Sancta Helena ora pro nobis
   for Petra Helen
   with much love from David
   Aug. 18th 1944.
   Mary was visited to redeem
   Eve, Helen was visited to redeem
   Emperors.
   Matins. Aug. 18th 2nd Nocturne. Lesson.
St Helena is shown with the Instruments of the Passion.

[111]

DRAWINGS & PAINTINGS

116 ABOVE THE AIRA BECK 1946
Pencil and watercolour, 19¼ x 24¼ (49 x 62.2)
Inscribed 'David Jones '46'
Private collection

In 1939 Helen Sutherland moved to Cockley Moor in Matterdale, above Ullswater. From this lonely house, 1,400 feet above sea-level, Jones painted his first landscapes since leaving Sidmouth in 1940.

*117 VIEW FROM GATWICK HOUSE, ESSEX, APRIL 1946
Pencil, watercolour and chalk, 18½ x 27 (47 x 68.6)
Inscribed 'David Jones 1946 from Gatwick House, Essex'
Private collection

116

118 KENSINGTON CHURCH STREET 1946
Pencil and watercolour, 13 x 8 (33 x 20.3)
Inscribed 'Ch St Ken May 24th 1946'
Catherine Dupré

Since October 1941 Jones had lived at 12 Sheffield Terrace, London W8, and it was there that he made this sketch of a girl who had passed back and forth several times, loaded with parcels.

119 THE TREE 1947
Pencil and crayon, 19 x 11½ (48.2 x 29.2)
Inscribed 'David Jones '47'
Mr and Mrs Christopher Hull

Drawn from Bowden House, Harrow, the nursing home in which he was treated for his nervous illness in the late summer months of 1947. Jones wrote from there on 24 August:
'I have to try and paint now. I paint trees from my window. It's part of the curative game, as, *in their judgement*, I've now reached a period when I *must* paint, because they maintain that my *major* conflict displays itself in relation to painting and it must be fought out in that terrain – that's not the whole story – but a very important part of it, *whatever* the inclinations, results, difficulties, feelings etc. etc.'
(*Dai Greatcoat*, p.134)

120 MY BRANCHES LOFTY 1947
Pencil and watercolour, 29 x 22 (73.6 x 55.9)
Inscribed 'David Jones 1947'
Mrs Rhoda Cowen

119

[112]

See no.119. Exhibited under this title at the Redfern Gallery, May–June 1948; in the Arts Council 1954–5 exhibition it was simply called 'The Tree' (no.60).

121 TYS ELVENLAND 1947
Watercolour, chalk and bodycolour,
29½ x 22 (75 x 55.9)
Inscribed 'David Jones 1947'
George Mitchell

See no.119. Title from James Joyce, *Finnegans Wake*, 1939, p.212

122 VEXILLA REGIS 1947
Pencil and watercolour, 29⅞ x 22 (76 x 55.9)
Inscribed 'David Jones'
Lit: H.S. Ede, *Agenda*, David Jones Special Issue, 1967, p.158
Kettle's Yard, Cambridge.

Drawn in October 1947. In a letter to Mrs Ede, Jones wrote:
'You have perfectly understood, in a remarkable way, much of the content behind the form of the picture. Yes, Rev[elation] 22:2 ['... on both sides of the river was the tree of life...'] certainly comes into it, though the main jumping-off ground was, I think, a Latin hymn we sing as part of the Good Friday liturgy in the Roman rite. Two hymns, in fact, one starting *Vexilla Regis prodeunt*, "Forth come the standards of the King" (written I think about the 5th century I think in Gaul), a very ancient processional hymn, in which are many allusions to the tree and the Cross, and to the Cross as a tree etc., and the other starting: *Crux fidelis inter omnes, arbor una nobilis*. This is a rather long hymn and in various of its verses deals with the Cross as a Tree in concise and very noble and moving language – really very grand. The robin you ask about: well there is that thing about the robin getting his red breast from the red drops from the Tree of the Cross. The general idea of the picture was also associated, in my mind, with the collapse of the Roman world. The three trees as it were left standing on Calvary – the various bits and pieces of classical ruins dotting the landscape – also older things, such as the stone henge or "druidic" circle a little to the right of the right-hand tree in the distance and then the Welsh hills more to the right again, the rushing Ponies are, more or less, the horses of the Roman cavalry, turned to grass and gone wild and off to the hills. (This idea, probably in turn, comes from something in Malory's *Morte Darthur* when right at the end, after the death of Guenevere and the break-up of the Round Table, Lancelot and other knights let their armed horses free to roam where they will – for the riders have now finished with tournaments, display, etc. and gone off to be hermits and the like.) The leopard's pelt and the trumpet in the left-hand bottom corner are supposed to be the instrument and insignia of a Roman *bucinator* or trumpeter, as though the owner of them had been part of the guard on Calvary – that sort of idea. The tree on the left of the main tree is, as it were, the tree of the "good thief", it grows firmly in the ground and the pelican has made her nest and feeds her young in its branches – Our Lord is likened to a pelican in her piety in one of the Latin hymns of Thomas Aquinas. The tree on the right is that of the other thief, it is partly tree and partly triumphal column and partly imperial standard – a power symbol, it is not rooted to the ground but is part supported by wedges. St Augustine's remark that "empire is great robbery" influenced me here. It is *not* meant to be *bad* in itself but in some senses proud and self-sufficient. Nevertheless it is shadowed by the spreading central Tree and the dove, in fact, hovers over this tree of the truculent robber for somehow or other he is "redeemed" too! I think that is about all. I should like to make plain that none of this symbolism is meant to be at all rigid, but very fluid – I merely write down a few of the mixed ideas that got into this picture as you were kind enough to ask. A Church dignitary once said to Lord Tennyson, with reference to a certain poem "Do these figures symbolize Faith, Hope and Charity?" to which Tennyson replied "They do and they don't and I don't like being tied down!" or words to that effect.

It's very like that in painting or any work of art, I think. So many confluent ideas are involved in a single image. It so happens that in this picture I have been able to "list" some of the ideas of the content for you. (It would be far less possible to do so in most of my pictures of course – at least far less easy – this picture is after all somewhat of an "illustration" as well as a picture. Not that it was deliberately so – it came like that.) – But they were less explicitly intended than perhaps it sounds, when written down, and there is much other stuff besides. It interested me

DRAWINGS & PAINTINGS

about your straight fir tree outside your window, because actually, of the trees which started me off on this picture, one was a pine and the other a fir (the other, I believe, a chestnut). They were outside my bedroom window in the nursing home when I was jolly ill for seven months – I did a number of drawings of those trees and then in the end did this complicated picture, very much influenced by the previous drawings, though quite different. The picture went through many vicissitudes, and suffered much alteration and was nearly torn up more than once. The psychiatrist, under whose care I was, *made* me go on, so that it was produced under rather special circumstances. (In a sense my doctor could be said to have been a "part-producer" I feel.)

A couple of other things relating to the picture: the nails with their ribbons were suggested by the Paschal Candle which, in Catholic churches, is lit during the Easter season. It is a very large candle and always decorated with flowers etc., and in the middle of it are inserted five separate grains of incense usually in little gilt containers, arranged in diamond formation, and although the actual history of this custom is very obscure, they are now taken to signify the Five Wounds of Our Lord. You mention also a Madonna, but I don't think there is one in this picture. The little female winged figure in the wood to the left, such as might be over a fountain – the guardian figure of the sacred well – that sort of notion – I think that was my idea of it.

P.S. Also of course the Yggdrasil of Northern mythology, the great tree with its roots far in the earth and its flowers in heaven no doubt comes into the picture – for all these things are one thing in some sense.'
(*Dai Greatcoat*, pp.149–152)

123 THE LORD OF VENEDOTIA 1948
    Pencil, chalk and watercolour,
    22 x 17½ (56 x 44.5)
    Inscribed 'Dafydd ab Jago me fecit Calan
    Mai 1948'
    British Council

For the role of this Lord as an Arthur/Christ figure see introduction pp.67–8. His history is summarized in a footnote to *The Anathemata*, p.72: 'It is generally accepted that the man known to Welsh tradition as

123

DRAWINGS & PAINTINGS

[115]

Cunedda Wledig was a Romanized Briton, almost certainly a Christian, and possibly associated with the office of Dux Britanniarum. Sometime before the year AD 400, he came, presumably under Roman auspices, from the district of the Otadini or Votadini in South Scotland, into Venedotia (N. Wales). His great-grandfather, his grandfather, his father and three of his nine(?) sons and one of his grandsons bore Roman names; two of which, Donatus and Marianus, are said to be certainly of Christian provenance. The rule which these men established for Wales, in the age of St Ambrose, was destined to evolve into a dynasty of native princes, which endured, in however precarious fashion, for nine centuries.'

There is a debt in the texture of this drawing, and in the proportions of the figure, to Henry Moore's graphic style.

124 TWO GIRLS OBSERVED AT MASS 1948
Chalk, 19 x 14 (48.2 x 35.5)
Inscribed 'David Jones, May '48'
Private collection

In 1948 Jones made many chalk drawings of the heads of girls. These works are comparable in spirit to the devotional diptychs of the Northern Renaissance, in which a portrait is paired with an image of the Virgin and Child. In the case of Jones's drawings the icon is omitted, but since the girls are attending Mass it is present by implication. A comparable drawing to no.124, of the previous month, is inscribed on the verso 'Child Observed at Mass+Le Maître de Moulins' – a clear indication of the Renaissance masters he had in mind. The mastery with which the black chalk and the colour are combined to achieve an open radiance of form reminds us of Jones's admiration for Holbein.

125 SUNDAY MASS: IN HOMAGE TO
G.M. HOPKINS, S.J. 1948
Watercolour, chalk and bodycolour,
22 x 15 (55.9 x 38.1)
Inscribed 'David Jones me fecit Whitsun 1948'
Private collection

The artist came to see the drawing some years after it had been sold: he sat in silence for ten minutes and then said 'Do you like the bird?' The inconspicuous little bird in the top left corner symbolizes, of course, the gift of the Holy Spirit at Whitsun. The dedication

124

DRAWINGS & PAINTINGS

reflects Jones's great love of Gerard Manley Hopkins; if he had a particular poem in mind it might well have been the hymn to Mary, *The May Magnificat*.

126 GIRL IN A HAT c.1948
Chalk, 22¼ x 15¼ (56.5 x 38.7)
Cyngor Celfyddydau Cymru
Welsh Arts Council

This most likely belongs with the 1948 series of heads, but it could date from a year or two later.

127 PRINCESS WITH LONG-BOATS c.1948 – 9
Pencil, crayons and chalk, 16 x 13 (40.6 x 33)
Scottish National Gallery of Modern Art, Edinburgh

This drawing was found in the artist's estate without any title or inscription: the crown suggests a queen or princess, the boats point to the era of the Arthurian legends and the stories of the *Mabinogion*. She may be Essyllt (Isolde). The style suggests a date not long after that of 'The Lord of Venedotia', perhaps 1948 or '49. The mysterious, metamorphic textures are again reminiscent of Moore's graphic style.

127

128 ECLOGUE IV 1949
Pencil and watercolour, 24 x 18 (61 x 45.7)
Inscribed 'David Jones '49'
Lit: *Word and Image*, no.112.
Helen Sutherland Collection

It was believed in the Middle Ages that a passage in Virgil's Fourth Eclogue foretold the coming of Christ. In this Annunciation to the Shepherds, the angel or sibyl points to the Eclogue lying open on the lap of the piper with the helmet of the First World War. Thus a parallel is drawn between the shepherds protecting their sheep from wolves and the soldiers in the trenches. Their meal is surely eucharistic, like the doling out of the issue tot in *In Parenthesis*:

> Come off it Moses – dole out the issue.
> Dispense salvation,
> strictly apportion it,
> let us taste and see,
> let us be renewed,
> for christ's sake let us be warm.
> O have a care – don't spill the precious
> O don't jog his hand – ministering;
> do take care.
> (p. 73)

128

DRAWINGS & PAINTINGS

129 A LATERE DEXTRO c.1943–9
Pencil, chalk, watercolour and bodycolour,
24½ x 18¾ (62.2 x 47.6)
Trustees of the David Jones Estate

This drawing, replete with symbolism, was begun from things seen. 'When at Sheffield Terrace David would go to Mass at the Carmelite church in Church Street (later destroyed by bombs). This, with memories of St Cuthbert's, Fr. John O'Connor's church in Bradford, provided the first scene for the series of poems grouped around the Kensington Mass, and for the idea behind the picture that was first known to some, at least, as "The Kensington Mass" and later as "A Latere Dextro". (The move to Harrow in 1947 brought a change of scene, in the picture, to the Church of Our Lady and St Thomas of Canterbury in Harrow.)'
(Dai Greatcoat, p.113)

On the basic theme of the drawing, the Mass as the renewal of Christ's sacrifice, see the introduction pp.58 & 65. The force of the title is explained by René Hague: 'Water issuing from the right-hand side is an image that he found particularly moving. It came to him from several sources: from the Dream of the Rood, v.20, where blood issues from the right: from the representation of the wound caused by the spear of Longinus, whence issued blood and water (the spear which dealt the dolorous stroke), traditionally shown on the right side; from Ezekiel's water issuing from the right hand of the Temple ...'(Commentary, p.167.)

Jones continued 'A Latere Dextro' over many years, and ultimately, in spite of passages of extraordinary vitality, overworked it.

*130 FLORA IN CALIX-LIGHT 1950
Pencil and watercolour, 22¼ x 30⅛ (56.5 x 76.5)
Inscribed 'David Jones 1950'
Lit: H.S. Ede, Agenda, David Jones Special Issue, 1967, p.157
Kettle's Yard, Cambridge

Between 1949 and the mid 1950s Jones made a large number of drawings of flowers in a glass chalice on a table in front of the window of his room in Northwick Lodge; see introduction pp.69–70. He liked to use 'Calix', Latin for chalice, in his titles because of its association with the botanical calix or calyx.

'I've only just tumbled to the simple scientific fact that "water" is the womb of all life – and of the simplest organisms – well that thrilled me no end – no wonder baptism is by water ... ' (Letter of 1943, Dai Greatcoat, p.122) That thought was certainly in the artist's mind when he drew the water in these chalices. A similar watercolour to this group (nos. 130–133) is described by Lord Clark:
'Some of the finest of David Jones's recent paintings are not of literary subjects, like Tristan and Isolde, but represent simply a vase of flowers on a table. A pleasant subject; but we are not for long under the illusion that this is an ordinary "still life". The vase, broad and capacious like a Byzantine chalice of the eighth century, stands facing us on a plain table. Although no exclusively Christian symbol is visible, we at once have the feeling that this is an altar, and that the flowers in some way represent parts of the eucharist. There are wine-coloured carnations and ears of corn, thorny stems of roses and blood red petals, which drop onto the small white table cloth. Yet none of this is insisted on, and we are far from the closed world of symbolism. Every flower is there for a dozen reasons, visual, iconographical, or even on account of its name, and how far they can be interpreted as Christian imagery no one, perhaps not even the painter can tell.'
(Agenda, David Jones Special Issue, 1967, pp.99-100)

131 CHALICE WITH FLOWERS AND SEAL c.1950
Pencil, crayon, watercolour and bodycolour,
30 x 22 (76.2 x 55.9)
Inscribed 'Dafyd J'
Cyngor Celfyddydau Cymru
Welsh Arts Council

See no.130.

132 MEHEFIN c.1950
Pencil, crayon, watercolour and bodycolour,
22¾ x 30½ (57.8 x 77.5)
Inscribed 'Dafyd J. Mehefin'
National Museum of Wales, Cardiff

See no.130. 'Mehefin' is Welsh for June – the month in which it was drawn.

133 GWYL DDEWI 1950
Pencil, crayon and watercolour,
26 x 29½ (66 x 75)
Inscribed 'David Jones 1950'
Helen Sutherland Collection

DRAWINGS & PAINTINGS

DRAWINGS & PAINTINGS

132

See no.130. The title is Welsh for Feast of David; daffodils, of course, being the flower of the patron saint of Wales. In the preface to *The Anathemata* Jones asked:

'If one is making a picture of daffodils what is *not* instantly involved? Will it make any difference whether or no we have heard of Persephone or Flora or Blodeuedd?

I am of the opinion that it will make a difference, but would immediately make this reservation: Just as Christians assert that baptism by water "makes a difference", but that many by desire and without water achieve the benefits of that "difference", so, without having heard of Flora Dea, there are many who would paint daffodils as though they had invoked her by name.' (p.10)

134

134 THE PASCHAL LAMB. ET VIDI AGNVM
    STANTEM TAMQVAM OCCISVM c.1951
    Pencil and watercolour, 18¾ x 14 (47.6 x 35.5)
    Nicolete Gray

'Generally I do not approve of explanations in words of what is meant to be shown forth visually in a drawing. But in this instance, I think, for a number of reasons, a note on the "content" of the drawing is, perhaps, justifiable. The Lamb, in accord with traditional iconography, carries a flag.

But in my drawing the flag is depicted as bent to a crossbar, as was the imperial *vexillum* of Roman imperatores of the later empire. The device XX derives from a different source. It chances that the 20th Legion was known as the Valeria Victrix. At the top of the upright half of the standard is a Winged Victory. Behind the figure of the Lamb is meant to be indicated the Seven-hilled Urbs seen, as it were, from the south-east, from a point where the Via Latina once made juncture with the Via Appia.

As certain of the Early Christian writers noted, that though the *viae* were constructed for strategic purposes, it so happened that they became the roads whereby the Cultus of the Order of Melchizedek was established beyond the narrows of the Fretum Gallicum in remote parts of this island far earlier, most like, than is usually supposed.

The foreground of the drawing is intended to indicate the stress and drag, tempest and ship-wreck of the world in general – the norm in fact as we know it.

DRAWINGS & PAINTINGS

The left foot of "the Lamb slain before the Foundation of the World" steps gently, lest the standing stones of a megalithic circle (the 'Henge if you like) are troubled. The drawing was made originally as an illustration to *The Anathemata* but was found to be not patient of reproduction; for one thing, colour was essential.'
(*Word and Image*, no.119)

135 LA BONNE BERGERE 1951
    Pencil and watercolour, $18\frac{3}{4}$ x 15 (47.6 x 38.1)
    Inscribed 'La Bonne Bergere David J '51'
    Lit: *Word and Image*, no.113
    Leicestershire Museums and Art Galleries

'This drawing was based on an aural tradition of a French family which was recounted to me in about 1950 by a descendant of the person concerned. The date according to family tradition was in Napoleonic times in the mountainous country of the French-Swiss border. It concerned the beating off of a wolf with the butt-end of a crook and blows from a wooden sabot. Tradition went on to say that the shepherdess returned to her homestead, but was deprived of her power to speak for months. Not a very surprising story in itself, but within a few days of hearing its relation, I chanced to read, in an English translation of a Latin classical author, "It is well known that wolves have the power to deprive men of their power of speech". No doubt, for fear can work marvels! But this witness from antiquity, coming so immediately on hearing the French girl's family tradition, inspired me to make this essentially illustrational drawing.'
(British Council tape, edited by Peter Orr.)

136 THE NECKLACE AND THE CALIX 1954
    Pencil and watercolour, 31 x 23 (78.7 x 58.4)
    Inscribed 'David J 1954'
    The Rt. Hon. Sir Hugh Fraser, MBE, MP

See no.130. The title given here follows the form of the Arts Council 1954 catalogue (no.74), rather than *Word and Image*, where it is listed as 'The Chalice and the Necklace' (no.125).

137 LA BELLE ENDORMIE c.1958
    Pencil and watercolour, 8 x $12\frac{3}{4}$ (20.3 x 32.4)
    Inscribed 'La Belle Endormie David J. circa 1958'
    Helen Sutherland Collection

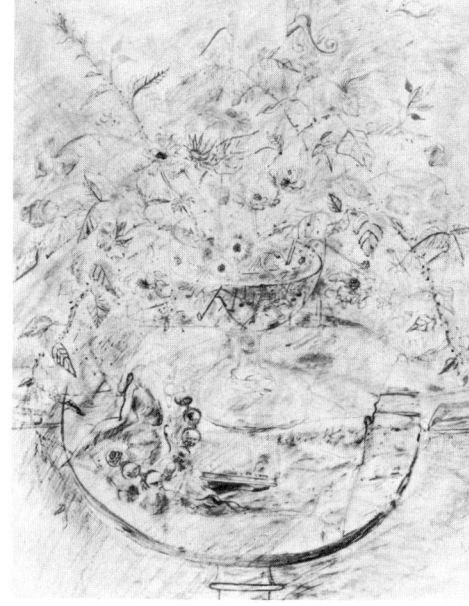

136

DRAWINGS & PAINTINGS

On the back are inscribed the signatures of the friends who presented it to Helen Sutherland, and a poem by Kathleen Raine.

138 GWENER 1959
Pencil and watercolour, 15 x 22½ (38 x 57.2)
Inscribed '$Ι ελρι γαρίαδ$'
Private collection

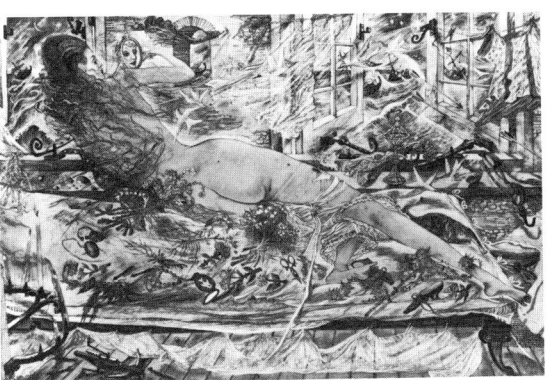

138

David Jones explained the picture in a letter to Valerie Wynne-Williams:
'As you know Aphrodite rose from the sea & there is the association between the seafoam-born goddess & Mars the war god so there is a sea battle in progress outside the room in which Gwener, Venus, Aphrodite (call her what you like) lies on what I suppose would be called in Welsh a Lleithig (straight from Latin Lectica a couch hence the classical form of the support at the foot-end of the couch). The wall of the ystafell is meant to resemble the usual form of Roman or classical building, layers of stone between layers of tiles or brick [revealed] where the covering plaster was cracked or fallen away. The hightide of the sea has flung up over the window sill some stones & shells & part of the tackle & cordage of one of the vessels smashed in the sea battle, & some ill-aimed or stray arrows from the battle also drive in through the open casement, on the ledge of which some of Gwener's vesture has been hung out to dry. Her tunica or dalmatic is hung on a bit of cord on the right side of the drawing, this garment, now worn only by assistant ministers at Mass was, in various forms, worn by all respectable citizens, men & women alike, in the later centuries of the Roman-Hellenic world.

The gulls as they sweep in become doves as they approach the goddess, because the dove was one of the creatures sacred to her. As you know, Eros or Cupid was the son of the Goddess and he carried a bow that discharged arrows. I decided that his bow should be a cross-bow & his arrows would be bolts, hence the cross-bow left under the couch & the bolts left on the coverlet mixed up with the flowers, lilies of the valley, love lies bleeding, roses and what not.

As for the wound in Gwener's thigh half bandaged – and I may be wrong about that, I had it in my head that Aphrodite or Venus was wounded in the battle at Troy – she being wholly on the Trojan side . . .

The cat at rest on the couch is because in the Nordic

[123]

DRAWINGS & PAINTINGS

mythology a goddess more or less equivalent with the classical Venus, had white cats that drew her car across the blue heavens, but I don't happen to much like white cats & so I made a tabby one or anyway a *cath brith*, anyway it was only an afterthought & an excuse to draw a cat.

The high-heeled shoe of Gwener I got from a watercolour reproduction of Lady Llanover's remarkably beautiful & detailed studies of Welsh costume of astonishing variety in the Wales of her day. That particular shoe was from Meirioneth. Scratched on the plaster in Greek letters the Welsh words TI ELRI LAN.'

139 CERDD DANT, CERDD DAFOD (String Song and Tongue Song) 1961
Pencil and watercolour, 19 x 14⅝ (48.3 x 37.1)
Inscribed 'Cerdd dant, cerdd dafod. Dafydd J. a'm gwnaeth.'61'
Julian Mitchell

Jones paired this drawing with an inscription that combined William Dunbar's poem

> Sing hevin imperiall most of hight
> Regions of air mak armony
> All fishe in flud and foull of flight
> Be myrthfull and mak melody

with the prophetic words from Virgil's Fourth Eclogue. The imperial and sibylline character of this angel is indicated by the purple laticlaves on the surplice. The inscription and drawing were published together as Faber & Faber's Christmas card for 1961.

140 STUDY FOR TRYSTAN AC ESSYLLT
c.1959–60
Pencil, watercolour and bodycolour, 29¾ x 22 (75.6 x 55.9)
National Museum of Wales, Cardiff

In the late 1950s Jones started work on another Arthurian subject, showing the fateful moment when Tristan and Isolde (in Welsh, Trystan ac Essyllt) drink the love potion on board ship. The moment when Jones had to abandon this his first drawing is recorded in a letter of 12 March 1960:
'... I'm struggling with my Tristan picture. I've transferred it now onto another piece of paper – which is a ghastly operation – but I could not do what I wanted with it on the original paper, and I did not want to lose the feeling of it by making the

140

endless alterations and adjustments which I wish to make...

The first one now becomes rather like the *natural scene* and the one I'm working on (see no.141) the actual "art-work" – the offering is the same, but under another mode, as it were... I don't know whether I shall pull it off – it's the hardest thing I have tried to do... I think it is because I have to find out so many, many things in some detail about the ship and its tackle. For my kind of drawing one *either* has to have the object *in front of one* – as flowers or trinkets or what not, or one has to find out the principle by which things work, helped out by memories of the sea and odd sketches, plus photographs, and not least, talks with dear Mick (Richey), that great navigator.'
(*Dai Greatcoat*, p.177)

DRAWINGS & PAINTINGS

141

DRAWINGS & PAINTINGS

141 TRYSTAN AC ESSYLLT c.1962
Pencil, watercolour and bodycolour,
30½ x 22½ (77.5 x 57.1)
unfinished
Lit: Kenneth Clark, *Agenda*, David Jones Special Issue, 1967, pp.97 – 8; Arthur Giardelli, *Agenda*, David Jones Special Issue, 1973/4, pp.50 – 3; R.L. Charles, *Amgueddfa*, pp. 9 – 12
National Museum of Wales, Cardiff

For the early history of this subject see no.140. In 1972 Jones recorded:
'Here, I wanted to get the feeling of a vessel at sea. Essyllt I saw as emerging triumphant, whereas Trystan, having drunk of the love potion which brings about the whole tragedy, realises what all this means. Below Trystan's right hand is a hunting horn, and he is releasing his beloved falcon. I wanted it to be neither light nor dark, not night, not day, but all of one tonality. It is St Bridget's Day, in the evening. Part of the constellation of the Bear, Arcturus, is seen in juxtaposition to the bear on the pennant flown from the foremast. I didn't put in the stars just because I thought they would look nice: I attempted to place them with the aid of one of those diagrams from a newspaper, showing the position of the stars for that month. This may sound rather absurd, but I must have something to go by. As I have said, the imagination takes off best from the flight deck of the known. There is a cat in the foreground: for one thing, I'm extremely fond of cats, and I've never known a ship that had not a cat aboard her. The ship is sailing from Ireland to Cornwall, into a head wind, which is blowing from the south-east, and there is an escort vessel near the top right of the picture. In the small boat on the left are a couple of Irish wolfhounds, intended as a present for King Mark – and that was about all he got out of the transaction!'
(British Council tape, edited by Peter Orr)

*142 Y CYFARCHIAD I FAIR (The Greeting to Mary) c.1963
Pencil, crayon and watercolour,
30½ x 22¾ (77.5 x 57.8)
Lit: Kenneth Clark, *Agenda*, David Jones Special Issue, 1967, pp.98 – 9; Arthur Giardelli, *Agenda*, David Jones Special Issue, 1973/4, pp.94 – 8
National Museum of Wales, Cardiff

Three themes are interwoven in this Annunciation in a Welsh hill setting: the turning of time at the moment of transition from the Roman to the Christian era; the Annunciation as symbolic of the Incarnation, and hence the Passion of Christ; and the reenactment of this Redemption of the world in the particular forms of Celtic myth. Gabriel is brother to Mercury; birds fly by his heels in allusion to the winged sandals of the messenger of the gods. His caduceus has become a sword, the sword of which the priest Simeon had said to Mary, 'Yea, a sword shall pierce through thine own soul also'. The pain of the Mother who will stand by the Cross is foreseen: a strand of the crown of thorns encircles the sword. In the sky the constellation of Virgo is in juxtaposition to that of Libra, the scales, whose form is like that of a cross. The ancient gods are failing, their columns are fallen; the Roman wolf (c.f. no.114) shelters in the skirts of the Virgin. She herself sits, holding the apple, a second Eve within her wattled enclosure, the *hortus conclusus*. Round about flows a brook, which is also her in sign: 'I, like a brook out of a river of a mighty water, I like the channel of a river and like an aqueduct come out of paradise' (Ecclesiasticus xxiv:41, see inscription no.165).

Mary is seen also in the figure of Olwen, of whom it is written in the Mabinogion, 'Yellower was her head than the flower of the broom, whiter was her flesh than the foam of the wave; ... Whoso beheld her would be filled with love for her. Four white trefoils sprang up behind her wherever she went ...' (Translated by Gwyn Jones and Thomas Jones, London 1949, p.111.) The animals and birds that Culhwch had to seek in his quest to win her – the ousel, the stag, the owl, the eagle and the salmon – are all to be found in Jones's drawing, for the quest of Culhwch is an allegory of the Passion of Christ.

THE INSCRIPTIONS OF DAVID JONES

The inscriptions of David Jones are an important part of his work, not just a side-line. He himself ranked them with his painting and his writing, as indeed a connecting link between these two, and one which gave him particular satisfaction. 'When they come off (and that's not all that often) they are much more satisfactory *to me* than most of my work'.

David Jones took to making inscriptions comparatively late in his career, after the publication of his book In *Parenthesis* and after the writing of much of *The Anathemata*. His early wood- and line-engravings include some lettering, two of his small boxwood carvings and his wall painting at Capel-y-ffin have passages of lettering; in the thirties he made a number of informal pieces to give or send as birthday or feast day greetings to friends, but it does not seem to be before the forties that he became interested in making inscriptions for their own sake. Now they become longer and more skilful. No.143 is a particularly successful example from 1945. The important break-through, however, comes about 1948 when he made a series of experimental inscriptions (including nos.144–7) which are different from any which came before, and which prepare the way for his mature work, which is again different.

The fact that David Jones worked with Eric Gill for a number of years, and was in many ways much influenced by him, makes it natural to assume that their attitude to lettering should be similar, since for both it was a major field of activity. In fact there is hardly anything in common. Gill was a letter-cutter and type-designer; when he carved, or designed lettering for carving, he accepted a job and the wording required. The beauty of the work is in the craftsmanship and the version of the roman letter which he evolved. As a type-designer he was concerned with the design of standard letters which could be combined into an infinite variety of words, which would be legible and widely useful. For David Jones on the contrary lettering was a 'private' art. He made his inscriptions for himself or occasionally as gifts. He made them at Christmas and sent photographs as greetings to friends, and he made them as illustrations to his own books. In a very few cases they were commissioned; but he always chose the text himself and treated it in his own way, disregarding for instance orthodox ideas of how words should be divided, and equally the difficulties which his technique presented for reproduction; with the result that some of those commissioned were never used for the purpose for which they were ordered. He was not in fact concerned with doing a job but with giving a visible, abstract form to the meaning for him of his text.

As an artist he wrestled with the problems of reconciling form and content, of working out a concrete, particular, coherent form, in words, or in colour, line and image, which should embody his consciousness; his sense of the past, always present, of the continuing, half-known process of Redemption, of our intermixed Celtic-classical inheritance. The tension is very obvious in the complexity of his later paintings and in the often obscure and perhaps overloaded quality of his writing. Lettering however of its very nature presented a simplification. Its material, words, are both abstract forms and conveyors of meaning. A phrase from the liturgy *gloria in excelsis Deo*, Glory to God in the highest, is not just a phrase from the Bible, it has connotations with the angelic host, with the making now of the birth of Christ at Christmas, and its celebration, with the Latin language and its association with the Roman Empire etc. These associations are therefore already present in the text which is therefore of fundamental importance. David Jones often wrote on the back of the inscription itself, or on the photographs of it, translations and references to his sources. I have therefore included these in the catalogue entries, using the artist's own translation wherever possible.

The words were the artist's starting point but their meaning had to be given a visual form, one which should be both abstract and evocative. Letters are legible, they are also adaptable. David Jones never studied lettering or its history, but he took over forms from various sources which came his way, Welsh and early medieval inscriptions, and Anglo-Saxon manuscripts, and used them when he found one which gave the flavour that he wanted. So certain forms are introduced in Welsh words, homely English is often in minuscule, Latin is more majestic (but never in orthodox Trajan letters).

Finally all these had to be worked into a unity. In the experimental group referred to earlier the artist tried out different media, wax crayon, pencil, watercolour. The background is made positive, it is part of the letters. In his work after 1950 it is no longer coloured – instead it is the letters which are coloured – but it is still positive, painted in in white. About 1956 he arrived at the technique which satisfied him. He painted the whole background over in thick Chinese white; he then worked over this, having made only a very rough pencil layout of his lines, usually underneath the white. He adjusted and re-adjusted, sponging out and overpainting on top of this until he had the movement and inter-relationship and feeling that he wanted, sometimes finally burnishing the surface 'which doesn't make it shiny, but it tends to further unify the forms'.

David Jones said that he was sometimes disappointed that his inscriptions looked so much alike. This is deceptive, the more one gets to know them the more individual they become. They are not examples of a style but unique expressions of the artist's reaction to his text. At first sight they look alike because they are expressive, not of diverse, exterior things or ideas, but of phrases which were fundamental to his whole way of thinking.

NOTE A good many of the inscriptions were dated by the artist on the work, or in the text inscribed, or on the photographs which he sent as Christmas cards. If however he was asked some years later to date a work, other evidence has shown that he could be several years out. These dates are therefore unreliable. v. nos. 144, 165.

The N.G. numbers given in the following entries refer to Nicolete Gray's catalogue *The Painted Inscriptions of David Jones*, London 1981.

143 QVIA PER INCARNATI 1945
Watercolour, 11½ x 8¾ (29.2 x 22.2)
Dated on the back 'Xmas 1945'
Lit: reproduced in *Motif* 7, 1961
N.G.7
Nicolete Gray

The text is from the Mass for Christmas, 'for by the mystery of the Word made flesh the light of thy glory has shone anew upon the eyes of our mind'. This is an example of an early informal inscription, made for a friend.

144 ROMA CAPVT ORBIS 1948
Pencil, wax crayon and watercolour,
10⅜ x 15 (26.3 x 38.1)
The inscription is dated 1949 in *The Anathemata* but this cannot be correct as it is referred to in a note (on the back of a photograph) dated 1948
Lit: reproduced in *The Anathemata*
N.G.14
Anthony d'Offay Gallery

The text 'Rome, head, splendour, hope of the world, golden Rome' is from a ninth century inscription. It expresses something of the artist's devotion to the Roman tradition. The use of yellow crayon is no doubt related to the golden shining implications of the text. This and nos.145, 146 and 147 belong to a group made in the late forties when David Jones started seriously working on inscriptions as an art form. They are all experimental in technique using different and mixed media for the letters and the background; both are positive elements.

145 HIC IACET ARTVRVS c.1949
Pencil on wax crayon, 22¼ x 17½ (56.5 x 44.5)
Dated by the artist c.1949
Lit: reproduced in *Motif* 7 1961
N.G.16
Anthony d'Offay Gallery

The text is from Malory's *Morte Darthur* 'here lies Arthur, the once and future king.'

This belongs, with nos.144, 146 and 147 to the group of experimental inscriptions made in the late forties. It is experimental both technically, pencil and wax crayon were never used in the later inscriptions, and in the letter-forms used which are here particularly wide and strong. R with a short leg and A without a crossbar never recur. Q with an interior tail and X with diagonal terminations are probably taken from reproductions of early medieval inscriptions seen by the artist about this time; he may also have had in mind the woodcut of the tombstone to Arthur shown in Camden's *Britannia* which has A with a bar on the apex. He was not, however, I am sure, trying to re-create an historic style, his reaction to the Romano-Celtic connotations of the Arthurian myth was much more personal and complex. David Jones made another, less interesting, inscription of the same text, about the same time (N.G.15)

146 OPTIMA MUSA 1948
Pencil on wax crayon scratched over with a blunt point, 15 x 11 (38.2 x 28)
A photograph of this inscription has a note on the back dated 31.XII.48, so it was probably made in this year, 1948
Lit: reproduced in *Signature* 8 new series, 1949
N.G.17
National Library of Wales, Aberystwyth

The text means 'Truth is the best Muse' written in alternate lines, Latin and Welsh. This is the strongest and most elaborate of the experimental group (see nos 144, 145). It is exceptional in lay-out with one word only to the line, in the way in which the background is worked, and in the very wide letter-forms. The use of special, more romantic letter-forms for the Welsh words, (U, A, E, N and D with a crossed stem) is a practice developed in later inscriptions.

147 GLORIA IN EXCELSIS 1948
Pencil, wax crayon and wash,
16 x 13 (40.6 x 33)
Signed 'D.J. fecit a.d. viii KAL IAN AVC MMLCCI'
The date given 2701 is from the foundation of Rome (Ab Urbe Condita) in 753, i.e. 1948
N.G.18
Anthony d'Offay Gallery

Photographs of this inscription were sent to friends for Christmas in 1948. The text 'Glory to God in the highest and peace to men of good will' is the song sung by the angels announcing the birth of Christ to the shepherds. It is also sung in the Mass on all feast days. This is the last of the early experimental inscriptions which use pencil and wax crayon.

INSCRIPTIONS

148 EXIIT EDICTVM 1949
    Opaque watercolour, 16 x 13 (40.6 x 33)
    Photographs of the inscription were sent as
    Christmas greetings in 1949 and it was no doubt
    therefore made in this year
    N.G.19
    Tate Gallery

The text is from the Gospel of St Luke 'There went forth a decree from Caesar Augustus' (that everyone should be enrolled), and she brought forth her first-born son and laid him in a manger, . . . and this shall be a sign to you'. The words round the side and top 'Apollo returns, now also the Virgin returns' are from Virgil *Eclogue* IV.

This inscription marks the beginning of a new phase in two ways. The coloured background and wax crayon technique are replaced by letters in different colours on white paper, heightened with white paint: this became the artist's regular technique, growing more finished and more elaborate in later years. Secondly, the artist here introduces his practice of combining fragments from different texts. This is really integral to his approach to these inscriptions. They give visual form to a complex of inter-related meaning. Typical here is the turning of the P of Apollo into the Christian Chi-rho symbol, echoing the interpretation of Virgil's line as a prophecy of the birth of Christ (a common medieval interpretation) c.f. no.159 and *Eclogue* IV (no.128), also of 1949.

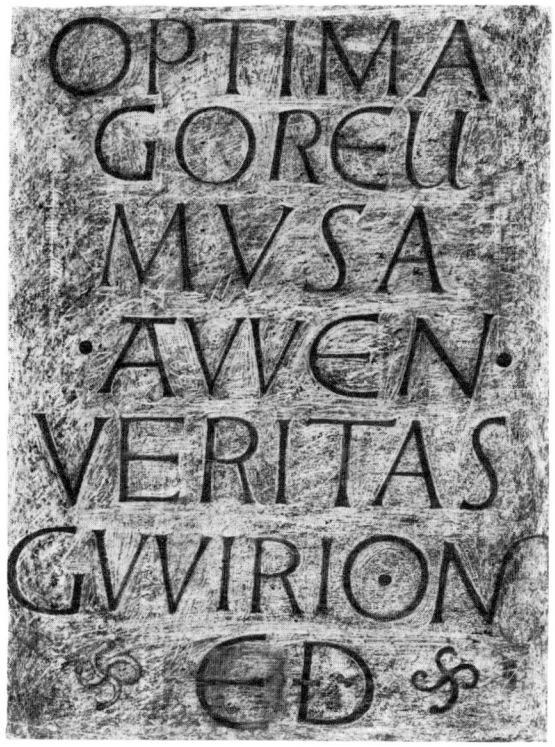

146

149 POSTEA SCIENS IESVS
    Watercolour and ink, 21⅞ x 15⅛ (55.5 x 38.4)
    Dated by the artist in *The Anathemata*
    Lit: reproduced in *The Anathemata*
    N.G.27
    Anthony d'Offay Gallery

The text is from the Gospel of St John which is chanted in the liturgy of Good Friday (called in Latin *feria VI in Parasceve*) by three cantors. The words inscribed are 'After this Jesus knowing that all things were now accomplished, in order that the scriptures might be fulfilled, said, "I thirst" '. The last word 'vas' is the beginning of the next sentence 'a bowl full of vinegar . . . ' sung by a different cantor, the narrator, (chronista). The inscription was made as an illustration to the artist's poem *The Anathemata* (p.237) where the paeon to Christ ends with 'his desiderate cry:

[130]

SITIO'. The author's note here says 'I found myself having to use the Latin "sitio" for the English "I thirst" because this is the form most impressed upon me by hearing the ministers singing the passion on Good Friday'.

150 ONGYREDE
   Watercolour, 19½ x 12 (49.5 x 30.5)
   Dated 1952 by the artist in The Anathemata
   Lit: reproduced in The Anathemata p. 240
   N.G. 28
   Anthony d'Offay Gallery

The text is from the Anglo-Saxon poem *The Dream of the Rood* and may be translated 'Stripped himself then the young man who was God Almighty, strong and courageous climbed he up on the high cross, proud in the sight of many, when he desired to redeem mankind'. This is the only inscription which is entirely in Anglo-Saxon and the artist has used various special letter-forms, some derived from Anglo-Saxon manuscripts, not to suggest any imitation of this style, but to convey his own feeling for the poem. The inscription was made for *The Anathemata* where it comes a few pages after POSTEA SCIENS IESVS illustrating the same final passage of the poem. Both were painted in two colours only because, unlike most of David Jones' inscriptions, they were made for reproduction.

*151 DVM MEDIVM SILENTIVM 1952
   Opaque watercolour on an under-painting of Chinese white, 19½ x 24¼ (49.5 x 61.6)
   Dated at the bottom 'on the feast of the nativity of Our Lord MCMLII'
   Lit: reproduced in Motif 7 1961; Arts Council catalogue 1954 no. 112; Word and Image, 1972 no. 152
   N.G. 30
   Victoria & Albert Museum

The text 'for while all things were in quiet silence and the night was in the midst of her course, thy almighty Word came down from heaven from thy royal throne' is from the Mass of the Sunday after Christmas (taken from the Book of Wisdom). It is echoed by the phrase round the edge from the carol 'I sing of a maiden'. This is the most elaborate inscription made by the artist hitherto, incorporating English and Latin, capitals and the more homely minuscule, and working them together into a complex pattern. Colour is used to heighten the significance of the words, green singles out 'Sermo', the living Word of God, purple the regality of his throne, yellow the radiance of heaven.

152 CHRIST EIN PASG early 1950s
   Watercolour, 7 x 12½ (17.8 x 31.7)
   There is no evidence of date; possibly the early fifties
   N.G. 33
   Private collection

The Welsh text means 'Christ our Pasch who was sacrificed for us, Alleluia'. This quite slight work was probably made as an Easter greeting for a friend; the artist made such pieces, sometimes very felicitous, from time to time, but they are different from the elaborate, finished inscriptions worked over, or painted on top of Chinese white and 'endlessly re-adjusted over the entire surface'. The patterned background in this inscription is unusually important, stars and dots etc. are quite often used in the early and informal pieces – to be distinguished from the dots used to separate words – and very occasionally in later inscriptions, such as no. 165, but the all-over pattern here seems to be unique.

153 ET EX PATRE NATVM 1953
   Opaque watercolour on an under-painting of Chinese white, 15¼ x 22 (38.7 x 55.9)
   Dated c. 1953 by the artist for the article for Motif. His dating was however often inexact. The lay-out suggests a connection with no. 154 dated 1956; the painting of the background round rather than underneath the letters and the persistence of Roman forms of R and Q however indicate a date before, not after, the latter inscription.
   Lit: reproduced in Motif 7 1961; Agenda vol. 5 nos. 1–3 1967; and vol. II no. 4 1973
   N.G. 35
   Anthony d'Offay Gallery

The first part of the text is from the Nicene Creed. '(Jesus Christ) born before all ages ... light from light ... begotten not made ... by whom all things were made ... and was made man'. The second part is from a prayer in the Christmas Mass 'By this most holy intercourse' (that is Holy Communion) 'may

[131]

INSCRIPTIONS

we be found in the form of him (Christ), in whom, in union with you (God) is the substance of our being'. By leaving out phrases in the Creed, known no doubt by heart by the artist and therefore rather implied than omitted, the inscription sums up the essence of the faith and hope of a Christian. The symmetry of the lay-out, and the restriction to black and significant red give a deceptively simple impression, in fact, the size, spacing and working together of the letters is the most complex hitherto.

154 PWY YW R GWR PIAV R GORON 1956
Opaque watercolour on an under-painting of Chinese white, $23\frac{1}{4}$ x $30\frac{3}{4}$ (59.1 x 78.1)
Dated on the back 'done in 1956'
Lit: reproduced in Motif 7 1961
National Library of Wales, Aberystwyth

The Welsh is from the medieval poet Gruffudd Gryg, 'who is the man who owns the crown the white God with this wound under his breast'. The Latin which follows is a literal translation. The second part begins with Latin 'a pure sacrifice, a holy sacrifice, an undefiled sacrifice' words said in the Tridentine Roman Mass just after the consecration. The Welsh is a translation. Both phrases therefore refer to our Lord, present at that moment, on the altar, and offered as victim and sacrifice.

This inscription, unlike any other, was designed to be enlarged and painted on the East wall of a Welsh convent chapel. In the event, the nuns found it too esoteric. Fortunately the artist painted the design as a finished inscription, indeed it seems to have been the first in which he used the technique which became characteristic, that of starting by painting over the whole surface of the paper in thick Chinese white, then working on top of this in colour. David Jones considered this as possibly his most important inscription. It marks the beginning of his mature period.

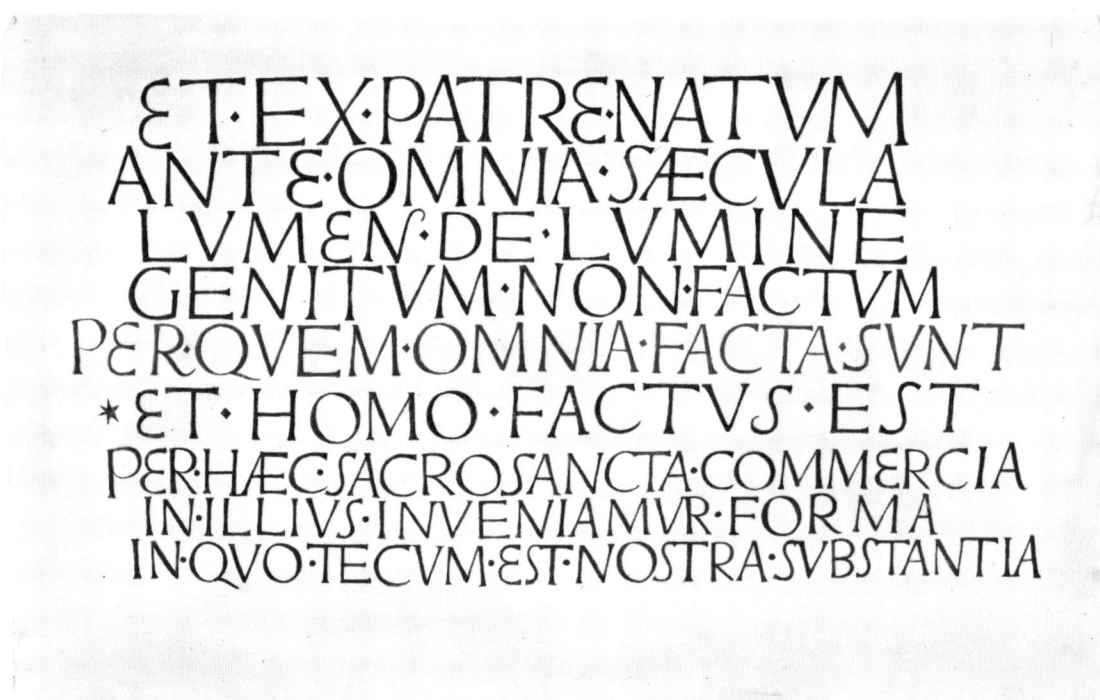

153

[132]

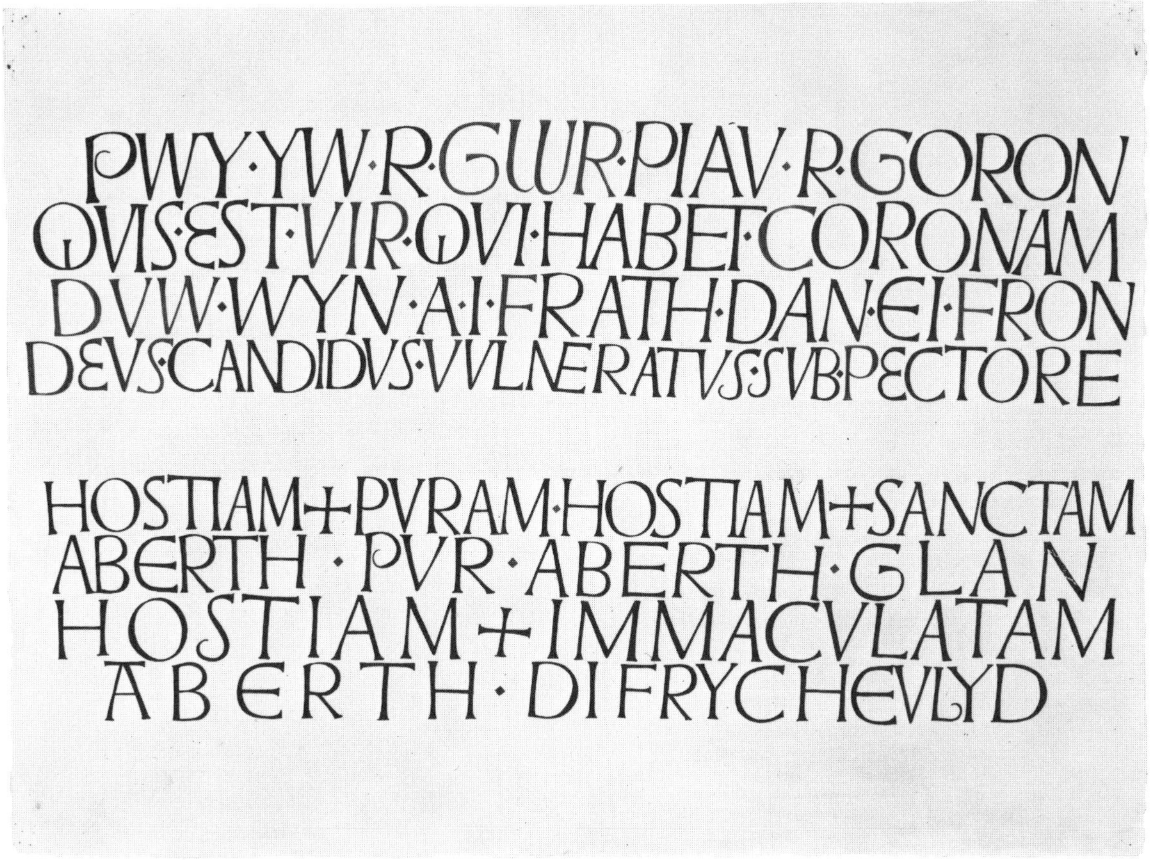

PWY·YW·R·GWR·PIAV·R·GORON
QVIS·EST·VIR·QVI·HABET·CORONAM
DVW·WYN·A·I·FRATH·DAN·EI·FRON
DEVS·CANDIDVS·VVLNERATVS·SVB·PECTORE

HOSTIAM+PVRAM·HOSTIAM+SANCTAM
ABERTH · PVR · ABERTH·GLAN
HOSTIAM + IMMACVLATAM
ABERTH · DI FRYCHEVLYD

154

*155 EX DEVINA PVLCHRITVDINE 1956
    Opaque watercolour on an under-painting of
    Chinese white, 18¼ x 15 (46.4 x 38.1)
    Signed and dated 'Dafyd J a'i wnaeth MCMLVI
    N.G.38
    The Countess of Avon

The Latin text is from St Thomas Aquinas 'All being is derived from the divine *beauty . . . nothing is in the mind unless first in the senses.' The English is from the translation of the *Roman de la Rose* attributed to Chaucer. The inscription was made for Clarissa, Lady Avon whose name appears in Greek letters at the bottom. This is one of a group of inscriptions made about this date for friends (nos.156, 157 and 158) all comparatively small, gayer than the bigger, more serious works, but equally finished and wonderfully rich in colour.

*The artist has misspelt the Latin in Devina and nehil.
 He did not worry much about spelling.

156 ACCENDAT IN NOBIS 1956
    Opaque watercolour on an under-painting of
    Chinese white, 10½ x 14½ (26.7 x 36.8)
    Dated July 12 1956 in the text, probably
    finished slightly later
    Lit: reproduced in *Motif* 7 1961
    N.G.40
    Mrs Adrian Bailey (née Sabina Grisewood)

The Latin is from the Tridentine Mass 'may the Lord enkindle in us the fire of his love and the flame of everlasting charity'. The English manages to combine

[133]

INSCRIPTIONS

the idea of the patronage of Sisley (Cecilia) with that of the grey-eyed Athene, in a typically allusive way. The inscription was made for Sabina Bailey (née Grisewood) for her confirmation. The same text was used again in an inscription of 1961 (N.G.60, and in an engraving in *The Ancient Mariner*).

157 PROPTER HOC RELINQVET HOMO 1957
Opaque watercolour on an under-painting of Chinese white, 15 x 20½ (38.1 x 52)
Signed and dated 'David J '57'
N.G.41
Lady Antonia Pinter and The Rt. Hon. Sir Hugh Fraser

The text is from the Nuptial Mass 'for this cause a man shall leave his father and his mother and shall cleave to his wife and they two shall be one flesh: this is a great sacrament.' The varied colours are typical of this group. Q with an interior tail, P with an inward curling bowl and A with a broken crossbar are characteristic of inscriptions from this date onwards. This was made for the marriage of Sir Hugh and Lady Antonia Fraser.

158 INGREDERE IN TEMPLVM DEI 1957
Opaque watercolour on an under-painting of Chinese white, 7½ x 10½ (19 x 26.7)
Signed 'David me fecit Rebeccae', dated in the text 1957
Lit: reproduced *Anglo-Welsh Review* 1972; *Word and Image* p.59
N.G.42
Rebecca Rose Fraser

The Latin is from the baptismal service 'enter into the temple of God that you may have part with Christ in eternal life'; and at the side 'to the fountains of water'. The inscription was made for Rebecca Rose Fraser for her baptism. A rather different sketch was made for this inscription which includes drawings of flowers. (N.G.43)

159 QVAERENS ME 1958
Opaque watercolour on an under-painting of Chinese white, 12¾ x 18 (32.4 x 45.7)
Signed 'Dyd digofaint ... Dafyd J a'm gwnaeth 1958' in pencil
Lit: reproduced in *Word and Image* pl.24
N.G.44
Trustees of the David Jones Estate

156

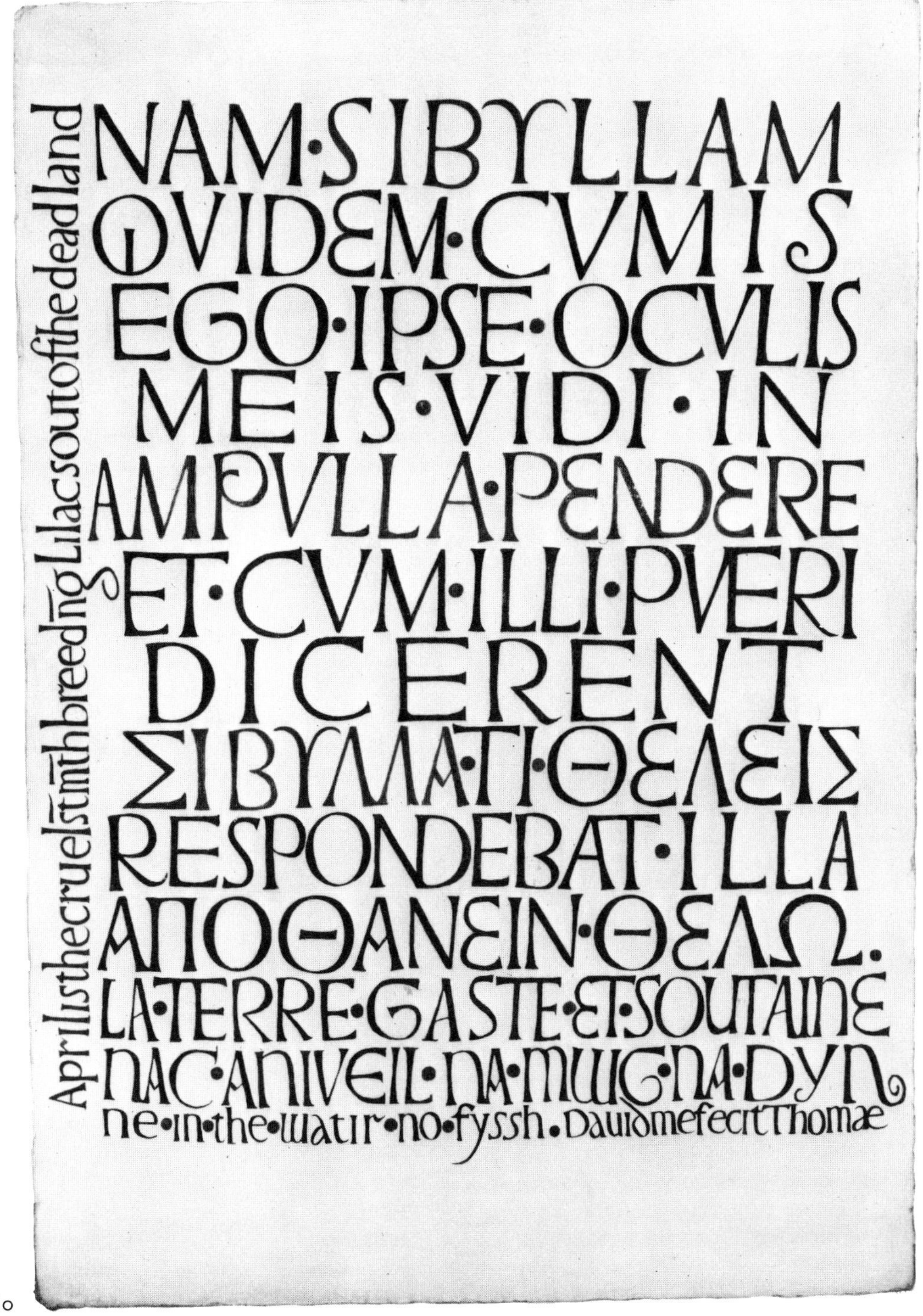

NAM·SIBYLLAM
QVIDEM·CVMIS
EGO·IPSE·OCVLIS
MEIS·VIDI·IN
AMPVLLA·PENDERE
ET·CVM·ILLI·PVERI
DICERENT
ΣΙΒΥΛΛΑΤΙ ΘΕΛΕΙΣ
RESPONDEBAT·ILLA
ΑΠΟΘΑΝΕΙΝ·ΘΕΛΩ.
LA·TERRE·GASTE·ET·SOVTAINE
NAC·A·NIVEIL·NA·MWCNA·DYN
ne·in·the·watir·no·fyssh·DavidmefecitThomae

Aprilisthecruelstmthbreedīng Lilacsoutofthedeadland

INSCRIPTIONS

The Latin is from the hymn 'Dies irae' which used to be sung at Masses for the dead. 'Seeking me you rested, weary, to redeem me you suffered the cross, let not that labour be in vain . . . on the day of the wrath, on that day the world will dissolve in ashes as was prophesied by David and by the Sybil'. The Sybil is another reference to Virgil's Eclogue IV (cf no.148). It appealed particularly to the artist's sense of the unity of the classical and Christian traditions.

The artist spoke about this inscription in his commentary on the slide series made for the British Council 'I happened to find an extremely beautiful piece of paper to begin with; that was a great help . . . it has almost the feeling of parchment . . . one I myself much like'.

160 NAM SYBILLAM 1958
    Opaque watercolour on an under-painting of
    Chinese white, 23½ x 16 (59.7 x 46)
    Signed in the text 'David me fecit Thomae'
    Lit: reproduced as frontispiece in *Symposium for T.S. Eliot's seventieth birthday*, 1958
    N.G.48
    Mrs T.S. Eliot

The inscription was made for T.S. Eliot and the text consists of passages about the waste land, a theme which fascinated David Jones. The first ten lines in Latin and Greek are from Petronius 'for the Sibyl of Cumae I myself saw with my own eyes . . . in the hanging vessel when the boys were saying "Sibyl what do you want", she answered "I want to die".' The medieval French is from *Parceval* 'the land waste and useless', the Welsh 'without animal or smoke or man' from *Manawydan son of Llyr*. The quotation on the last line is from Malory's *Morte Darthur* and that down the side is the first line of Eliot's poem *The Waste Land*.

161 BEIRD BYT BARNANT 1958
    Opaque watercolour on an under-painting of
    Chinese white, 23¼ x 15¼ (59 x 38.7)
    Dated on the back 'made between August 28 and September 5 1958 by D.J.'
    Lit: reproduced in the artist's collection of essays *Epoch and Artist* and probably made for this purpose
    N.G.47
    National Library of Wales, Aberystwyth

Lines 2 and 4 translate the Welsh taken from the medieval poem Y *Gododdin*. The Latin, from *Ecclesiasticus* was translated by David Jones 'but on the judge's seat they shall not sit . . . yet with the creation of the everlasting ages they (in some sense) collaborate, and their prayer is in the operation of their art, and without these the city is not built'. So, in some sense, this is a statement of David Jones' assessment of the function of the poet-artist.

162 WHAT SAYS HIS MABINOGI 1958
    Opaque watercolour over an under-painting of
    Chinese white, much worked over,
    30 x 22½ (76.2 x 57.1)
    Signed Dafyd J a'm gwnaeth. Photographs sent as a Christmas greeting in 1958
    N.G.45
    National Museum of Wales, Cardiff

'Mabinogi' tale of infancy; the text is about the contrast between the infant Christ, 'born by the wayside' and his Godhead proclaimed in many tongues, Alpha and Omega, Atheling, prince, of the Heaven king, harrower of Hades, leader and high priest, ruler of the heavens, and Walda, ruler of every land. The Welsh and Latin words round the sides and bottom are a Christmas greeting 'blessed Christmas, in many places, in many ways'. The text is from *The Anathemata* p.207, where the allusions implicit in the various titles are noted; here they have been given visual expression not just in the introduction of different letter-forms in the Celtic and Anglo-Saxon words, but in every detail of form, spacing and juxtaposition concentrated into this multivocal paean.

163 CARA WALLIA DERELICTA 1959
    Opaque watercolour on an under-painting of
    Chinese white, much worked over,
    23 x 15¼ (58.4 x 38.7)
    Signed in pencil 'Dafyd J a'm gw'th 1959'
    Lit: The inscription was made for *Wales through the Ages* edited A.J. Roderick, where it is reproduced in Vol.I; also in *Agenda* David Jones special issue, 1967
    N.G.49
    National Library of Wales, Aberystwyth

The text is a lament for the death of Llywelyn ap Gruffydd, Prince of Wales, killed in battle in 1282. The text is from two medieval Welsh poems and

cara·Wallia·derelicta
ÐVGWYL·DAMASEVS
BAB·YRVNVEDDIÐAR
ÐEG·OVIS·RAGFYR
DVW·GWENER✝
AC·YNA·I·BWRIWYD
HOIL·GYMRY
Y'R·ILAWR·VENIT·SVMMA·DIES
ET·INELVCTABILE·TEMPVS
DARDANIÆ·PENN·DRAGON
PENN·DREIC·OED·ARNAW
PENN·LLYWELYN·DEG
DYGYN·A·VRAW·BYT·BOT
PAWL·HAEARN·TRWYDAW.
ab·hieme·añ·1282

(left margin, vertical): NYT·OES·NA·XYNGOR·NA·XLO·NAC·EGOR.

from the description of the fall of Troy in the *Aeneid*. 'Dear Wales abandoned, on the feast day of Pope Damasus, the eleventh day of December, a Friday; then was all Wales cast down to the ground, our latest day, the inevitable hour of Troy has come; a leader's head, a dragon's head was on him, head of fair resolute Llywelyn; it shocks the world that an iron steak should pierce it. Since the winter of the year 1282 there is no counsel, no lock, no opening'. The crowded letters, their strange, sometimes awkward shapes, and the painful over-working of texture all convey the sense of tragedy.

164 DEWI WYNFYDEDIG 1959
  Opaque watercolour on an under-painting of
  Chinese white, 6 x 9½ (15.2 x 24.1)
  Signed and dated 1959
  N.G.48
  Private collection

'Blessed David pray for beautiful Elri, March 1'. Made for Valerie Wynne Williams for the Feast of St David.

165 MVLIER CANTAT 1960
  Opaque watercolour on an under-painting of
  Chinese white, 22¾ x 15 (57.8 x 38.1)
  Signed 'Dafyd J'; on the back is written 'made
  about 1962'. It was however used as a
  Christmas card in 1960, so must have been
  made in that year
  N.G.55
  Anthony d'Offay Gallery

The text is a mosaic of references to Our Lady and the Incarnation; from James Joyce (the first two words), the Bible (Ecclesiasticus), and William Dunbar. The Latin and Welsh may be translated 'the woman sings . . . I, like a brook out of a river of mighty waters . . . I, like the channel of a river, and like an aqueduct, came out of Paradise . . . God was the Word and the Word was made flesh. He that ye might not come to, to you is come full humbly'.

*166 VERE DIGNVM 1961
  Opaque watercolour on an under-painting of
  Chinese white, 15½ x 21½ (39.4 x 54.6)
  Signed 'David J Feb 1961 sol in piscibus'
  N.G.56
  Helen Sutherland Collection

The artist has reverted to the use of a rich variety of colour to enhance the meaning of the text, which unlike most of the late inscriptions, is taken from one source, the Preface, the great thanksgiving prayer in the Mass. 'Truly worthy and just it is, right and at one with our salvation to render thanks at all times and in all places (to God) : alpha omega : . . . with the angels and archangels and together with the whole host of the heavenly war-band'. The inscription was made as an eightieth birthday present for Helen Sutherland.

167 CELESTIALL FOWLIS after 1955
  Opaque watercolour, 7 x 8½ (17.8 x 21.6)
  No indication of date
  N.G.58
  Jack Sweeney

The forms of R, G and A suggest that it is almost certainly after 1955. The looped M occurs also in SYNG HEVIN the inscription made for a Christmas card for Faber and Faber in 1961. The text also in both cases is from Dunbar of the *Nativitie of Christ*. A date about this time therefore seems most likely.

168 EXTENSIS MANIBUS 1964
  Opaque watercolour on an under-painting of
  Chinese white, 22½ x 16¼ (57.1 x 41.3)
  Signed in pencil, 1964
  Lit: A colour reproduction was made by the
  Curwen Press.
  N.G.61
  Peter Levi

This inscription was made for the ordination of Peter Levi. It is therefore about the Mass and includes phrases from the Canon and the rubrics of the Mass. It may be translated 'with extended hands he proceeds with these (offerings) which You vouchsafe to accept as (You accepted) that which was offered to You by Your high priest Melchizedek; gifts of the god of wine (liber) and the spirit of water (Naiades) poured out of the corn godess (Ceres); broken in an effective recalling of Him who freed the waters and established Your greatest sacrament in the substance of water.' This is one of the three last inscriptions made by David Jones.*

*Very interesting comments on the making of this inscription may be found in letters from David Jones given by Peter Levi to the Bodleian Library, Oxford.

GRATIAS AGIT DEO EXTENSIS MANIBVS
PROSEQVITVR QVÆ
ACCEPTA HABERE
DIGNERIS SICVTI
QVOD TIBI OBTVLIT
SVMMVS SACERDOS TVVS
ΜΕΛΧΙΣΕΔΕΚ
MVNERA OF LIBER ET
NAIADES: POURED OUT
OF CERES: BROKEN
IN ANAMNHΣIΣ OF HIM
WHO FREED THE WATERS
ET QVI MAXIMA QVÆQVE
SACRAMENTA IN AQVARVM
SVBSTANTIA CONDIDISTI
SACERDOS ORDINATVS PETRVS LEVI E SOCIETATE IESV

168

MANUSCRIPTS

The selections from the manuscripts of In Parenthesis and The Anathemata have been lent by the National Library of Wales, Aberystwyth. A detailed catalogue of the manuscripts of In Parenthesis and The Anathemata, by Daniel Huws and Philip W. Davies, will be published shortly by the National Library.

169 'IN PARENTHESIS' Part 7

Successive drafts of the passage printed on pp.176 – 7. The final manuscript of this passage is missing. Six or seven preliminary drafts exist for a large proportion of In Parenthesis.

170 'THE ANATHEMATA'

The passage from the earliest surviving draft of The Anathemata which was to become the opening of the printed version (p.49). National Library of Wales, cat.A1. folio 1.

171 'THE ANATHEMATA'

Two sheets from the second draft, including poetry printed on pp.235 and 237, and notes on p.238. National Library of Wales, cat.A2.ii, folios 232^V and 233.

172 'THE ANATHEMATA'

Three sheets from the final manuscript, printed text pp.137 – 9. In this passage Jones describes a ship symbolic of the Crucifixion and the argosy of mankind (c.f. introduction pp.46–7.) National Library of Wales, cat.A7. folios 6,7 and 8.

BIBLIOGRAPHY

BOOKS BY DAVID JONES

In Parenthesis, Faber, London 1937.

The Anathemata, Faber, London 1952.

Epoch and Artist, Faber, London 1959.

The Sleeping Lord and Other Fragments, Faber, London 1974.

The Kensington Mass, Agenda Editions, London 1975.

The Dying Gaul and Other Writings, Faber, London 1978.

Introducing David Jones, ed. John Matthias, Faber, London 1980; selections in paperback from *In Parenthesis*, *The Anathemata*, and *The Sleeping Lord*.

The Roman Quarry, Agenda Editions, London 1981.

SECONDARY LITERATURE
(Works devoted to Jones exclusively as a writer have been omitted)

Arts Council of Great Britain: David Jones, An Exhibition of Paintings, Drawings and Engravings, Cardiff 1954.

David Blamires, *David Jones, artist and writer*, Manchester 1971.

R.L. Charles, 'David Jones – Some Recently Acquired Works', *Amgueddfa: Bulletin of the National Museum of Wales*, 22, (1976) pp.2–13.

Kenneth Clark, 'Some Recent Paintings of David Jones', *Agenda*, David Jones Special Issue, vol.5, nos.1–3, (1967) pp.97–100.

Douglas Cleverdon, *Word and Image IV* (Catalogue of the exhibition arranged by the National Book League), London 1972.

H.S. Ede, 'The Visual Art of David Jones', *Agenda*, David Jones Special Issue, vol.5, nos.1–3, (1967) pp.153–8.

Arthur Giardelli, 'Three Related Works by David Jones', *Poetry Wales*, David Jones number, vol.8, no.3, (1972) pp.60–71; reprinted in *Agenda*, David Jones Special Issue, vol.11 no.4 – vol.12 no.1, (Autumn/Winter 1973/4) pp.90–8; and in *David Jones: eight essays on his work as artist and writer*, ed. Roland Mathias, Llandysul 1976, pp.88–100.

Arthur Giardelli 'Trystan ac Essyllt by David Jones', *Agenda*, David Jones Special Issue, vol.11 no.4 – vol.12 no.1, (Autumn/Winter 1973/4) pp.50–53.

Eric Gill, 'David Jones', *Artwork*, no.23, (Autumn 1930); reprinted in *Essays by Eric Gill*, London 1947, pp.147–53.

Edmund Gray, 'The Representational Painting of David Jones and Ben Nicholson', *Agenda*, vol.12, no.4 – vol.13, no.1, (Winter/Spring 1975) pp.126–34.

Nicolete Gray, 'David Jones', *Signature*, N.S. no.8, (1949) pp.46–56.

Nicolete Gray, 'David Jones and the Art of Lettering', *Motif*, no.7, (Summer 1961), pp.69–89; reprinted in *Agenda*, David Jones Special Issue, vol.5, nos.1–3, (1967) pp.146–52.

Nicolete Gray, introduction to *Helen Sutherland Collection*, Arts Council Exhibition, London 1970.

Nicolete Gray, *The Painted Inscriptions of David Jones*, London 1981.

René Hague, *David Jones* (Writers of Wales), Cardiff 1975.

René Hague *A Commentary on the Anathemata of David Jones*, Wellingborough 1977.

René Hague (editor) *Dai Greatcoat: A self-portrait of David Jones in his letters*, London 1980.

Paul Hills, 'The Romantic Tradition in David Jones', *The Malahat Review*, 27, (1973) pp.39–80.

Paul Hills, 'The Radiant Art of David Jones', *Agenda*, Special Issue on Rhythm, (1972/3) pp.125–37.

Paul Hills, *David Jones 1895–1974*: Catalogue of Exhibition at Anthony d'Offay Gallery, London 1979.

Robin Ironside, *David Jones* (The Penguin Modern Painters), London 1949.

Ruth Pryor (editor), *David Jones: Letters to Vernon Watkins*, Cardiff 1976.

John Rothenstein, *Modern English Painters. Lewis to Moore.* London 1956, pp.289–309.

BIBLIOGRAPHY

Peter Strevens, 'David Jones and his "bits of lettering"', *Anglo-Welsh Review*, vol.22, no.50, (Autumn 1973) pp.58–64.

For further bibliography see the book by David Blamires; also Samuel Rees, *David Jones: An Annotated Bibliography and Guide to Research*, New York 1977. Recent additions are regularly noted in the *David Jones Society Newsletter*, edited by David Blamires at the Department of German, The University, Manchester M13 9PL.

TAPE RECORDING
In 1972 Peter Orr made for the British Council a tape recording of David Jones talking about his paintings and inscriptions.

LIST OF LENDERS

Aberystwyth, National Library of Wales 29, 101, 146, 154, 161, 163, 169–172
Mrs Francis d'Abreu 104
H. R. Allen 43
Lady Helen Asquith 106
Countess of Avon 155

Mrs Adrian Bailey 156
Barnsley, Cooper Gallery 76
David and Camilla Bosanquet 107
British Council 97, 123
T. F. Burns 36, 67, 113

Cambridge, Kettle's Yard 51, 122, 130
Cardiff, National Museum of Wales 7, 14, 20, 31, 34, 35, 54, 65, 75, 91, 99, 100, 132, 140, 141, 142, 162
Lord Clark 83
Douglas Cleverdon 1–6, 8–13, 15, 17, 58, 90
Mrs Rhoda Cowen 120

Anthony d'Offay 27, 42, 62
Anthony d'Offay Gallery 144, 145, 147, 149, 150, 153, 165
Catherine Dupré 70, 118
Kulgin Duval 24

Edinburgh, Scottish National Gallery of Modern Art 127
Mrs T.S. Eliot 160

The Rt. Hon. Sir Hugh Fraser 136, 157
Rebecca Rose Fraser 158

Arthur Giardelli 80
Miss M. L. Graham 68
Nicolete Gray 84, 134, 143
Guild of St Joseph and St Dominic 26
Peter Guy 69

Philip Hagreen 19
Colin H. Hamilton 24
Professor C. J. Hamson 82
Thomas Hodgkin 72

Edgar Holloway 30
Miss Jaqueline Hope Wallace 39
Sir Antony Hornby 95
Mr and Mrs Christopher Hull 48, 94, 119

Trustees of the David Jones Estate 129, 159

Leicestershire Museums and Art Galleries 135
Peter Levi 168
Liverpool, Walker Art Gallery 77
Loftus Collection 32
Museum of London 55
The Trustees of the late Mrs F. H. Low 89
The late N. B. C. Lucas 64, 88

George Mitchell 121
Julian Mitchell 139
Barbara, Countess of Moray 52

Newcastle-upon-Tyne, Laing Art Gallery 114
Newport Museum and Art Gallery, Gwent 63

Lady Antonia Pinter 157
Portsmouth City Museums and Art Gallery 33
Private collection 16, 18, 25, 44, 45, 46, 47, 49, 50, 57, 59, 61, 71, 85, 86, 102, 105, 112, 116, 117, 124, 125, 138, 152, 164

Michael Richey 74, 103
Richard Smart 79

Helen Sutherland collection 41, 66, 73, 78, 81, 87, 93, 96, 98, 128, 133, 137, 166
Jack Sweeney 167

Trustees of the Tate Gallery 28, 60, 108–111, 148
T. L. Taylor 38
Mrs D. Tegetmeier 21–23, 40, 115

Victoria & Albert Museum 56, 92, 151

Welsh Arts Council 126, 131
Whitworth Art Gallery, University of Manchester 37, 53

PHOTOGRAPHIC CREDITS
David Clarke
A. C. Cooper
Prudence Cuming Associates
Michael Duffett
Michael England
Cecilia Gray
Ben Johnson
David Lambert
David Nye
Photo Studios Ltd
John Webb